EMPOWERING STUDENTS

Seven Strategies for a Smart Start in School and Life

Robert Brower
Amy Keller

Rowman & Littlefield Education
Lanham, Maryland • Toronto • Oxford
2006

Published in the United States of America
by Rowman & Littlefield Education
A Division of Rowman & Littlefield Publishers, Inc.
A wholly owned subsidiary of
The Rowman & Littlefield Publishing Group, Inc.
4501 Forbes Boulevard, Suite 200, Lanham, Maryland 20706
www.rowmaneducation.com

PO Box 317
Oxford
OX2 9RU, UK

British Library Cataloguing in Publication Information Available

Library of Congress Cataloging-in-Publication Data

Brower, Robert, 1951–
  Empowering students : seven strategies for a smart start in school and life /
Robert Brower, Amy Keller.
     p. cm.
  Includes bibliographical references.
  ISBN-13: 978-1-57886-491-1 (hardcover : alk. paper)
  ISBN-13: 978-1-57886-492-8 (pbk. : alk. paper)
  ISBN-10: 1-57886-491-7 (hardcover : alk. paper)
  ISBN-10: 1-57886-492-5 (pbk. : alk. paper)
  1. Motivation in education—Handbooks, manuals, etc. 2. Character—Study
and teaching—Handbooks, manuals, etc. 3. School children—Conduct of life.
I. Keller, Amy, 1977– II. Title.

  LB1065.B778 2006
  370.15'4—dc22

                                                          2006006808

⊗™ The paper used in this publication meets the minimum requirements of
American National Standard for Information Sciences—Permanence of Paper
for Printed Library Materials, ANSI/NISO Z39.48-1992.
Manufactured in the United States of America.

What Is Success?

The definition of success
To laugh much;
To win respect of intelligent persons
And the affections of children;
To earn the approbation of honest critics
And endure the betrayal of false friends;
To appreciate beauty;
To find the best in others;
To give oneself;
To leave the world a little better
Whether by a healthy child, a garden patch, or a redeemed social condition;
To have played and laughed with enthusiasm
And sung with exultation;
To know even one life has breathed easier because you have lived—
This is to have succeeded.

—Ralph Waldo Emerson

CONTENTS

APPENDIXES

PREFACE

All educators struggle to find the perfect solution to the seemingly complex problems of building character and promoting success with their students. Most teachers are constantly seeking propitious ways to reach all students, either behaviorally or cognitively—indeed, strategies that will transform students into successful students with good character. *Empowering Students: Seven Strategies for a Smart Start in School and Life* delineates how teachers can transform their teaching style so that every student has the necessary tools to become successful both in school and in life.

Empowering Students takes a profoundly different approach to motivating students to achieve and become successful. Most authors who write motivational books propose actions teachers must take to control and motivate students to learn and behave. This book focuses mostly on classroom behavior and success. We want to stress the importance of illustrating how these strategies can be applied in life and in the classroom. Students are often given tools to become successful students but not successful adults and citizens. In addition, the strategies can be shared with other students so they too can become not only victorious in a classroom environment, but victorious in their careers, relationships, and other facets of life.

This approach is an attempt to empower teachers to take control. It includes advice on strategies teachers should undertake that will change behaviors in students—a behavioral approach to correcting negative behaviors and actions that prevent learning from taking place. This book takes a somewhat different approach to the same problems and adds some surprising twists and approaches that illustrate the seven strategies that can change their lives forever.

This approach is vastly different from previous ideas simply because teachers and administrators will give students the power to change themselves to become successful in every classroom, not just for the teacher who has mastered the strategies espoused in this book. Once students change their perceptions of what is necessary to become successful, nearly all will respond in positive ways.

Through the implementation of these strategies, a profound change in behaviors and attitudes will follow, leading to more success in school and in life. Students will see how these strategies can influence their behaviors both in the classroom and in situations in their lives outside of school. Ultimately, positive character traits will evolve as they master the art of understanding and then implementing the seven strategies. Students will become motivated to promote their own success like never before. Administrators and teachers will see drastic changes in students.

This book has 11 chapters, seven of which reflect each of the strategies. The remaining chapters outline basic concepts related to the seven strategies as well as summarize major points within this book. Teachers and administrators will learn how to convey these strategies in much the same way they have been reaching students for decades. The information in this book is neither complex nor difficult to implement. We offer here commonsense ideas with practical applications that have proven highly effective with those who have implemented them.

There is a legendary story of Christopher Columbus about a conversation with the nobles who had organized a banquet in his honor after returning from his voyage to the new world. The courtiers sitting around the banquet table were making comments about how the discovery of the new world was no special feat and that anyone with sailing skills could have made the same discovery. Columbus, without directly responding to his detractors, asked those at the table to take a hardboiled egg that was nearby and try to balance it on its end. After all the courtiers failed to balance the egg on end and the egg finally returned to Columbus, he simply tapped the end of the egg on the table, slightly denting the end, and the egg successfully balanced on its end. The courtiers began laughing and commented that anyone could have balanced the egg doing what Columbus had just done, to which Columbus replied, "Isn't it amazing how simple it seems once we know the answer to the problem."

This story illustrates a very important lesson regarding simplicity for all administrators, teachers, and students. Success in life or success in any adventure can usually be traced to simple procedures, facts, or ideas. This is why this book is so effective in helping students to grow in highly positive ways. The strategies are simple, but profound, in effect, just like Columbus's discovery of the new world.

Although we do not profess to know all the answers to complex problems, we do, however, believe the answer to helping students to become successful is not as difficult as some would have us believe. For example, Sir Isaac Newton's law of motion and reasoning can be reduced to simplistic notions of just a few laws; music is based on just a few basic notes; all the colors of the world can be made using just the three primary colors (red, yellow, and blue) and black and white; television sets use only three colored lights to illuminate the world's colors; there are only four tastes we can distinguish; there are only five senses in the human body in which we are aware; most experts agree humans only exhibit seven emotions; the English alphabet consists of only 26 letters; there are only four nucleic acids in our DNA strain; to learn a foreign language, most experts agree that 500 words will do the trick; Lincoln's Gettysburg Address had fewer than 400 words (of which most were one syllable); there are only two sexes; and thousands of other similar simplistic notions make our world a beautiful place.

In other words, ideas do not have to be complicated to work. Ideas and concepts can be simple in context and simple to implement. Simplicity is an idea that most students will embrace. Students have so many avenues in their lives that are complex in nature (i.e., social opportunities, academic success, goal-setting, etc.). They wholeheartedly embrace a process that is simple not only in organization but also in implementation. By learning a few straightforward strategies, any student can build positive character and learn how to be successful in school and in life.

Although it is no secret what works in reaching children, some have outlined a prescription that is highly effective in reaching all students. One of the simplistic secrets of success is developing the skills necessary to build and sustain strong, positive relationships. One chapter in this book addresses this strategy specifically, but the book has an overriding theme of relationship-building sustainability that uses six other powerful strategies to complement this idea.

If all the information expounded in this book were put into a "pill" form, one could call it the "success pill." Since no "pill" exists that can be swallowed with an ensuing success story, then one is left with words of profound advice that will work just like the "pill." Those words of practical wisdom are the seven powerful strategies revealed in this book.

This book is filled with interesting stories and vignettes that will entertain you as you become immersed in the strategies. You are encouraged to reflect on the stories, strategies, and messages put forth and develop your own stories and strategies to pass along to students. Students who read this book are encouraged to look at their own lives and reflect upon previous experiences so they, too, can produce a positive attitudinal change.

In addition, it is highly encouraged to take notes, highlight phrases, and continually reflect upon how these strategies can become a part of building profoundly positive relationships with students to ensure their present and future success in school and, more importantly, in life. Use this book as a working notebook for your ideas, thoughts, and reflections. Then, bookmark stories, quotes, and anecdotes. We encourage the educator to format his or her own implementation strategies for the seven strategies presented.

There have been thousands of kids who have benefited from the words in this book through our talks and teachings on the subject of success and character building. Rarely does a month go by that we do not hear from a former student who calls or writes to say a word of thanks for passing along the strategies of sagacity. This book is dedicated to those students. It is hoped that this book will touch millions more students. The message is simple and easy to apply. It requires no money and anyone can do it. It is as simple as that! Good luck to the reader of this book in the pursuit of a successful life . . . it begins anew today.

INTRODUCTION

Every student can learn, just not on the same day or in the same way.

—George Evans

It is our hope that teachers and administrators will use this book to help students become motivated to learn and be successful both as students and adults. We also recommend first reading the book in its entirety to get the "big picture" of what is being espoused. Since this book is unique in its approach to motivate students, the educator should reflect on each strategy and make notes on how best to teach a particular strategy. Although the methodology used in this book is one of stories, lectures, informal talk, and discussion, the readers must develop their own methodologies for delivering this important information.

This section begins with a story of a young man who transformed his life in middle school. This story is true, but the circumstances and names have been altered somewhat to protect the person. This story forms the basis for everything that follows in this book. However, there are many students we have taught or administered that represent similar success stories. After reading the story presented here, we will begin to examine the seven strategies developed as a result of this story that will help students become motivated, develop a successful winning attitude, and build character in school and in life.

We have many real-life stories that illustrate how each of the seven strategies applies to real people. Because we cannot give real names and places of actual people and situations, we have changed the stories so as not to resemble documented situations. The message behind the stories remains, but the stories used have been fictionalized. Any similarities to actual people or events are strictly coincidental and are not intended to even remotely resemble any real-life person, place, situation, or event.

The stories offered are embellished fictions or analogous happenings to stories that others have told us. You should strive to see why the story is being told relative to the strategy involved and to grasp the message and not simply remember the stories.

Some of the stories that appear throughout this book are extreme cases, and thus the message might be disturbing to some readers. We have discovered that by using powerful stories and examples, students become more immersed in the message and heed the message conveyed by the story so that the student is motivated to take strategic action. These stories are a metaphoric mirror placed in front of the students so that they can see themselves as the possible reflection of the story exhibited in the example. Here is my story as a first-year teacher and how I handled a situation with a very troublesome student.

Sitting at my teaching desk peering outside my large classroom windows into the cold darkness, I seemed transfixed, almost hypnotized, as the new workday was about to begin. It was January 8, and a light snow was falling outside my middle school art classroom window. I was awaiting the flood of students pouring down the hallways beginning a new semester. The holiday break was over, and I was looking forward to seeing the students again. I found myself excited, yet apprehensive at the same time. I was happy to see the kids again, but sad to say goodbye to two full weeks of vacation (with pay). This is a feeling only a schoolteacher would understand.

Thoughts swirling around in my head swiftly turned to thinking about the new students I would encounter this first period of the day. More importantly was the question of what attitudes the new students would exhibit in each of my six new classes. I had quickly learned that one or two behavior problems can make life miserable for any teacher, let alone a fledgling mentor, like me. The bell rang and I quickly made my way to the door where my students would soon be entering my classroom. It was time; time to get ready for the youth of America. I knew I was ready for the new nine weeks of instruction.

Before I could reach the door to the hallway, Joe bolted into my room. My first thought was how could this student get here so fast, when the bell had just sounded. Joe was a seventh-grade student I knew by name but not by face—until now! When I asked him his name, he shouted, "Joe, but you probably already know me!" A stunned silence gripped me as I realized who the infamous "Joe" was. A sick feeling engulfed me as I told myself that, as a professional, I had sworn a Hippocratic oath to service all who enter my classroom. This would be my greatest test yet as a young teacher.

Joe had developed a sordid reputation with the teachers and administrators that was nothing short of miserable and disastrous. As a sixth grader the previous year, he had set records for suspensions and office discipline visits. In addition to this, Joe had been expelled from school for a severe disruption on the school bus. It seems he was caught drinking whiskey from a pint bottle on his way to school.

Not only had he not learned any lessons from the previous year, but it appeared he was becoming bolder and more popular with the other renegades. When school started in the fall, Joe had returned but was under strict guidelines. He was required to report to the office every morning directly from the bus. Just before the bell rang each day, he was given permission to go to his locker and then directly to his first-period class. That was why Joe was first to my class this fateful morning.

Now, Joe stood before me, and the rush of uncertainty created goose bumps over my arms and legs. I found myself asking, "Why me?" Knowing I couldn't do anything about his attendance in my class, I swallowed hard and resolved to make the best of a bad situation. After all, this is a public school; he probably had an attendance problem, and I still had 15 sick days remaining on my contract. I figured in a worst case scenario I might see him only 25 days out of 45 possible for the 9-week grading period.

My last fleeting thought was that I was not alone, six other educators had to experience the same malady as me; the fortuitous thing was at least I would have him out of the way first thing in the morning. Perhaps doing construction work would be a better profession? After all, anything might be better than what I was about to encounter with Joe.

When Joe entered the classroom, he had no notebook, no pencil, and no need for a seat close to the front. I figured he didn't want to be close to me, the enemy. I managed a quick and less than enthusiastic, "Welcome to art class. You will need to get a sheet of paper from off the top of my desk and help yourself to a pencil as well. We will be going over the required supply list and you will need to make a list of these supplies." Joe's response was alarming. He said, "Whatever! Is your name Brower? My friend says you suck." I retorted, almost embarrassed, "Joe, I don't suck, and you are never to use that word in this classroom ever again. Is that understood?" A snorting laugh was all I heard.

Luckily, the class was filled with excited kids, several of whom were excited to be in my class again. As the classroom filled, Joe's table had three empty seats, and I had three standing girls. They had eyed Joe (and the three empty seats near him) as they walked in toward the end of passing period. I walked over to them, smiled, and whispered, "It will only be for today." They smiled politely back and said, "Thank you, Mr. Brower."

The girls seated themselves strategically around the three sides of the table, as far away from Joe as they could get. They had no more than sat down when he began kicking at one of the girls, all while sliding down into his seat. I tried not to watch the girls as they sat down, but I could not ignore the muffled words, "Quit it, quit it!" Joe seemed oblivious to the fact that I was walking briskly toward him. He was entirely consumed with trying to kick Becky, and I appeared as a simple annoyance to his task. I reached his chair and pulled back on it quickly, which deposited him quickly onto the floor.

Everyone seemed amused until they realized I was serious and was ready to strike a further blow to his rancorous misbehavior. Joe slowly and methodically rose to his feet without a word; he glared at Becky as though he could kill her. He then turned his gaze to me. Without saying a word, I walked to my desk and retrieved the piece of paper and pencil I had requested all students to acquire. I continued to give instructions as I walked to Joe and deposited the items in front of him, hoping the behavior would cease.

I began going over the needed supplies for the class and could hear a tip, tap, tip, tap which became increasingly louder and more annoying.

Within seconds, the tip tap of the pencil became a full-scale percussion work. Exasperated and exhaling all the air in my body, I turned once again, walked over to Joe, and simply pulled the pencil from his hand and stared at him for what seemed like an eternity.

The stare was more of a disgusted look than a threatening pose. Joe blurted out, "Why did you do that? Give it back to me. You said you wanted me to write stuff down." I stated very sternly, "Joe, please, let us just get through this and we'll talk after class." He went off into a tirade about how I was picking on him, and how he knew that he wasn't going to like my class. Incredulous, I simply returned his pencil and continued discussing with the class the required subject supply list. Two minutes must have passed and I sneaked a glance to see what Joe was doing. I could see he was doodling on the paper, lost in subconscious thought. I felt a sense of release and hopefulness.

My hopes were quickly doused; he leapt to his feet and began wadding his paper with both hands, while violently proclaiming, "Three, two, one, the shot's off, and it's no goooooood!" He had missed the wastepaper basket by 20 feet. He now marched up to the desk for a second sheet of paper. On the way, he said, "I made a mistake on the last piece." Trying to keep myself composed in the middle of a firestorm, I told myself to remain calm.

Glancing at the clock on the wall, I realized only 4 minutes had passed since the class began. As Joe pranced to my desk to get a new sheet of paper, he also grabbed a plastic ruler I had on my desk. He took it, almost inviting me to say no! On the way to his desk he flipped Jeremy on the back of the head with the ruler. Jeremy simply leaned forward as if it hadn't even happened. Joe laughed and muttered, "Sissy."

By now, my blood was beginning to boil. In addition to this, Joe landed himself in his chair and managed to move the desk nearly a foot. Joe grabbed the table edges and moved it violently back into position; he began to run the serrated edge of the plastic ruler up and down the side of the desk making a loud zipper noise. I turned and yelled at the top of my teacher voice. "I have had it with you! One more incident and you will be out of here for good! Do I make myself clear young man?" Joe said nothing.

As I turned away from Joe, I began looking out the windows. Because it was pitch dark outside, the room reflected in the window as a giant mirror. As I looked into the reflection, I noticed Joe's image pumping his middle finger in the air directly at me. He was mouthing, "Take this you a°#h@°!." Joe was totally unaware I could see his near perfect reflection in the window. I stopped in my tracks and jerked around to face him. His finger was still pumping in the air. Dumbfounded, he realized I knew what he was doing and placed his entire hand into his pant's pocket; he turned away, hoping I would somehow ignore what had just taken place.

At that moment, I felt my body temperature rise. Almost in slow motion, I jumped over a chair between Joe's location and mine as the paper I was holding flew from my grip and floated aimlessly toward the floor. I sprung to Joe's seat arriving with such force that I had to use his body to keep me from falling forward. Joe, meanwhile, was lost in his ruler fun. Startled, Joe flung back and put his hands to his face to protect himself. I instinctively reached out for Joe's arm to lift him out of his seat. The grip on Joe's arm was secure enough to lift him from his seat. My secure grip caused Joe to writhe in pain. As I pulled Joe outside the classroom, I released my firm grip, and he fell to the floor.

As he landed on the tiled floor, I poked my finger continually into his chest as I re-created his horrible behavior just 11 minutes in. I was so upset with Joe that my words were spitting saliva in the air. At that very moment and as I looked at Joe's eyes moist with tears, I saw a little boy scared and remorseful. Joe attempted no retaliation toward me. All he did was make a whining noise while saying, "I'm sorry, I'm sorry, I'm sorry."

Suddenly, a gripping fear of remorse came over me. What had I done? Would I lose my job over this? How could I possibly let a 13-year-old child get me this worked up? Could I get sued? Was his dad bigger and tougher than I was? What must my class be thinking? What kind of a teacher was I? I stepped back from Joe and stood up. Joe was sobbing and looking down at the floor. As I lifted him up from the floor, he gave no resistance.

Inside my room, I could see the stunned look on my students' faces. I reached around Joe's shoulder to put my arm around him and said, "Let's go to the bathroom to get ourselves together." We both walked as I began my apologies. "I am so very sorry Joe, but why in the world would you do all of those things to make me so angry?" Joe whimpered simply, "My dad hit my mom this morning and I've been upset ever since I left the house. It wasn't your fault this happened Mr. Brower; I deserved it." At that very point, I had a defining moment in my professional life. I would never be the same person, the same educator again.

I returned to class and instructed Joe to stay outside the room until I came for him. I apologized profusely to the kids, almost full with self-pity. The remainder of the class period passed quickly; just a minute before the bell rang, I went out to see Joe. He would not look at me. I said I was sorry once again and told him I was wrong and that tomorrow we would start anew. I patted him on the back and said, "Have a good day." The bell rang and I stayed in the hallway to say goodbye to the kids leaving class. Most students left by way of the other hallway door, to assuredly avoid any possible eye contact with me. Now it was time for round two with my next class. What would follow?

The remainder of the day went off without a hitch, but the memory of first period would never go away, not that day or the rest of my teaching days. I made up my mind that if I were going to stay in the teaching profession, I had to figure out a way to reach all of my students, not just the motivated, but the unmotivated as well. I thought to myself that there would be more "Joes" who would come into my classroom every year who would need me to make a difference in their lives. Could I do it? Would I do it? Was this profession for me? The answer to all three questions soon became a resounding "yes" and what follows is what transformed from that very incident.

This incident is what created the strategies outlined in this book for promoting success and building positive character in all students. The strategies presented here have grown in stature and importance over the years. We teach these strategies to each student we are exposed to, whether in the classroom or in any other situation that might lend itself toward this type of meaningful discussion.

We have presented these strategies to other schools, factions, and athletic teams that want their students to succeed. The coaches and teachers who have implemented the strategies claim that no single technique has been more effective in helping kids be successful in school and in life. In point of fact, we have not experienced any other method that has proven more effective in helping students become better people.

The message delivered in this book is historical, universal, and time-less. The message is not new; it was formed from the annals of human behavior into a package that is easy to use and costs nothing to implement. Those who put the strategies delineated in this book to work will reap enormous benefits. Students can expect better grades, better relationships, more happiness, and, ultimately, more success in the classroom and in life. Their character will be enhanced in profoundly positive ways.

When Joe came to class the next day, I greeted him with a smile and a handshake. He returned the favor. I was relieved to have a second chance with Joe and my other students and asked Joe to stop by after school to talk. He graciously said he would. After school that day, I simply tried to find out as much as possible about Joe. It was surprising to me how much he opened up to me about anything and everything important to him. We must have talked for 2 hours without interruption.

The next day, Joe was at my door 5 minutes early for class and wanted to talk. Joe announced he would be staying after every day to talk and to help around the room, and he did. With each passing day, progress was being made. The turning point in Joe's life, however, was not just my interest in him, but rather in learning about and implementing the strategies for success espoused in this very book.

Teaching these strategies is the essence of this book and is at the core of how to reach all students. We convey the seven strategies in the form of discussion/lecture/informal talk. This powerful message has been taught to well over 10,000 students. The delivery of the strategies is usually given in two segments over 4 days. Two full hours (usually 2 days of class time) are devoted to the first six strategies, usually presented on the second and third days of each term. The last strategy of the seven is reserved for the end of the term and the talk lasts approximately 2 hours (usually 2 days of class time). The appendices in this book also give several ideas, organizational methods, and ways to successfully implement these strategies. No matter which method is chosen, it is sure that the effect will be profound with all students!

How a teacher conveys the strategies is dependent upon the comfort level of the teacher or administrator. Although we use a discussion, lecture, informal-talk format, full of various personal stories and school-related examples, any good teacher can develop implementation procedures that work best for his or her own class.

Joe heard my talk the second and third days of class and then, at the end of the 9 weeks, strategy seven was addressed. After the first talk, Joe stayed after class and stated that this had been the best talk he had ever heard. Unbeknownst to Joe, he was the reason I gave this talk in the first place; it was directed at him, but others quickly articulated they enjoyed it as well.

The night after my unfortunate run-in with Joe, I resolved to do something to help the Joes of the world. These strategies of success were born, and this book is an attempt to share the message in a much broader venue with supporting research that complements this process.

Joe was so enraptured by the message, he begged me to let him get out of another class to hear the talk on the strategies for success again and again. Not surprisingly, four teachers agreed to let him out of their classes to come to my class to hear the talk four more times. That year, Joe heard the talk five times in 9 weeks. As Joe progressed through his eighth-grade year, he was sent to the office only one time for a minor incident. Throughout the school year I began to hear teachers make positive remarks about Joe; that was an incredibly defining moment in my understanding of the power of presenting the advice outlined in this book!

During Joe's freshman year, he was in the school play and volunteered every time a student was needed. His homeroom class won the door-decorating contest at Christmas, and Joe had done all the artwork. He had taken up drawing cartoons for the school newspaper, and in the spring he was elected to the high school senate.

Joe is now an account executive working for a large corporate paper company. Joe must have listened to the seven strategies talk on more than 30 separate occasions. He claimed he never got tired of hearing the message and the stories. In addition to this, Joe imputed his improved behavior and attitude to the enlightening message of these strategies.

In the Summer 2005 issue of *The Master Teacher*, editor Robert De-Bruyn wrote "that the most powerful statement you can make to students" is to simply convey as a teacher/administrator that I "believe in you" as a student (DeBruyn, 2005). This powerful message can transform nearly any student, but, in particular, the students like Joe who may well need us the most. As you begin reading this book, keep in mind the simple belief in all students regardless of how difficult that might be, because by doing so, we open the gates of a very rewarding career in education.

1

BUILDING THE FOUNDATION FOR THE SEVEN POWERFUL STRATEGIES

There is an extensive list of sources in the references section of this book. The most compelling aspect of reading and researching the books listed as resources for this narrative writing is that all of the books basically say the same thing. The only difference is scope, package, and methodology of implementation. This book takes a somewhat different approach to helping students empower themselves so that they can be successful in any setting and not just in the classroom of enlightened teachers. We truly believe and preach the strategies found in this book. The success of our students has been, in a large part, because of the strategies developed in this book.

A quick look at the several biographical similarities follows here with other sources listed in other sections of this book. The point made here is that the research is quite similar on: what motivates students, how to manage a classroom to ensure learning is taking place, what type of instructional practices work best to keep students engaged and learning, what methods to employ to keep students from acting out in class, what goals can be used to motivate students, how to project caring in the classroom, how to prevent drop outs, and how to connect with students and parents in the learning process.

The wealth of information in the myriad books on this very subject continues to be rewritten. As you begin the journey of reading what works best in this book, we encourage you to seek the relationship between what the research is saying and what is being espoused in this book. Although not every idea, thought, opinion, or belief has a sourced resource, one can find those ideas backed in the pages of the books and articles listed in the references section of this book.

To define the term success, one must venture to many books, articles, research-based journals, and other texts, which might help you better understand this term. It is curious to know that the word success is found in only one verse in the entire Bible. This verse, Joshua 1:8, finds God promising Joshua that he would have great success if Joshua were strong, courageous, and obedient (Rice, 2004). Success might also be defined as achieving high levels of integrity, courage, and patience. A successful school, as defined by Dr. William Purkey and John Novak (1996) in *Inviting School Success*, involves a school where the environment is inviting, safe, and proactive, and where students think deeply about personal and social concerns, basically a school that is democratically oriented.

In addition to these descriptions, *Merriam-Webster's Dictionary* defines success as a favorable or desired outcome; the attainment of wealth, favor, or eminence. As you can see, success is a difficult term to precisely define. We prefer the term success to be applied differently to each and every student. Success to one student might be turning in all of his or her homework assignments in one 6-week term; success to another student could mean a 4.0 grade point average. Educators must remember that each student is individual in his or her successes, but the educator should continue to utilize this talk in each and every aspect of school and in life. The application to both is critical to student achievement.

Character is an even more difficult word to meticulously define. Using similar resources, character can be defined in terms of actions, behaviors, voice, or written sources. Character is defined, using *Merriam-Webster's Dictionary*, as a person of moral excellence and firmness. Stephen Covey (1998) relates three terms to the word character: integrity, maturity, and abundance mentality. All of these terms collectively are the foundation of his Fourth Habit: Think Win/Win. In addition to these authors, Elaine McEwan (2003) claims one of the *10 Traits of Highly Effective Principals* includes being a character-builder. This in itself requires an educator to be a role model who is trustworthy, who is respected, and who has integrity.

In using these resources to more accurately define character, we are satisfied with the final definition. Any definition describing character must surely contain the words trustworthiness, respect, and integrity. We, too, see the importance of these words in defining character. Students and teachers/administrators should embrace this definition of character and strive to better their own character traits to encompass these three terms.

Donna Tileston (2005) writes in her book titled *Ten Best Teaching Practices* that students need to learn to set personal goals so they are motivated to achieve and learn and to act positively in class. She also notes the importance of using differentiated instruction to make learning more individualized.

Sheryn Northey (2005) states in her book *Handbook on Differentiating Instruction for Middle and High Schools* that the real key to instructional effectiveness is to differentiate instruction, hence, students are highly motivated to achieve and learn. Much of the handbook overlaps what Tileston says in her book. The key idea is that students can be motivated by the simple approaches a teacher takes to instructing.

Likewise for Cheryl Gholar and E. Riggs's (2004) book on *Connecting with Students' Will to Succeed: The Power of Conation*. They write about the need to teach students to want to learn and succeed, and that making the content interesting will make the material relevant, which will motivate students to persist in the learning process, much like Schlechty (1997) advocates in his book.

Finally, Randi Stone (2005) writes in her book titled *Best Classroom Management Practices for Reaching All Learners* that collecting strategies that award-winning teachers use in their classrooms will promote effective classroom management and facilitate learning. She, too, finds very similar ideas that permeate the entire spectrum of successful practices. Among these are using effective classroom management skills to handle students so they might learn better. Successful teachers often use a community mindedness in their outlook (DuFour & Eaker, 1998); they often have procedures when rules are broken; they use a wealth of diverse approaches and settings; they use cooperative learning; and they use relevance to keep the students motivated in the subject matter being learned.

As we begin to set the foundation and you learn about the first strategy to teach students, remember the goal is to teach the student to be his or her own empowered person, to teach the students to take control of his or her own life in highly productive and effective ways. In this section of the book, the use of the *success pill* and the *failure model* are discussed. These two items set the stage for what is to follow and build the foundation with students, which gets students in a frame of mind to actively listen and learn.

Administrators and teachers must assess each student to determine if a given student is capable of being motivated. We believe every student can be motivated to learn and to be successful in life. It is imperative to assess students who are failing academically to determine if the student "can't" learn the necessary skills or "won't" learn the necessary skills. The first group presents unique challenges to all educators and rarely is this group a problem behaviorally, *unless* they have a severe disability. The second group, the "won't" group, are the students who often manifest behaviors and attitudes that are hurdles to their future success.

This book is targeted at the "won't" group, because this is the group that confounds educators and can make our lives miserable at times. We believe and have experienced near total success in reaching every student we have encountered in this very group. However, this book is not just about these "won't" students, the message is aimed at all students, and the results are largely the same.

Barbara Reider's (2004) book is an excellent source to explore some of these same topics on how to help students behave properly and structure the classroom to help students succeed. Reider states that classroom management is a key ingredient in helping students to be successful in school, as is a nurturing, caring, and peaceful climate. Additionally, Reider writes about empowering students, rethinking teaching so teachers become facilitators of learning versus givers of information. In addition, teachers must build a classroom (school) environment conducive to rapport building and cooperation among all adults and students in the school environment. Lastly, Reider writes that rules must be clearly stated to students, effective procedures put in place to ensure the rules are followed, and clear-cut consequences delineated in the procedures. Understanding these ideas will help you understand why these concepts are so important as a foundation to empower students to succeed.

Administrators and teachers must also realize that we can no longer count on every parent to fully support our efforts (Rogers, 2004). In today's world, children are faced with all types of adversity, including a lack of guidance at home. Parents can be divorced, separated, absent, incarcerated, addicted to drugs (illegal or prescription), mentally and physically abusive, mentally unstable, addicted to alcohol, dead, or may simply not care about the well-being of their children. Therefore, it is paramount that educators and schools become the oasis for children— a safe haven, indeed, a place where they feel safe, trusted, cared for, and loved. This has to be nurtured and demonstrated daily on the part of all adults in the school. Some children will come to school to feel love— often, for the first time.

Once students are confident that they are in a caring environment where the adults are there to help them, then the child can begin to trust adults and take these behaviors and skills beyond school and into life's situations (Deiro, 2004). Our ultimate goal is to free children from the bondage of failure and open up a world to them that they have yet to experience, or even imagine. Once the light of enlightenment is shining brightly, the child begins to grow in profoundly positive ways. The seven strategies for success is the approach we have used to successfully communicate the strategies that are paramount to truly motivate all students to build positive character and become successful.

The stories offered here are simply personal examples we use in our own talks. You will quickly discover that when you tell your own stories to students, you, too, will have the undivided attention of the student. Stories are incredibly powerful ways to communicate important information. As we all know, Abraham Lincoln and Mark Twain were masters of the "story" and helped to shape both written and oral anecdotes.

Although we present the information in the teaching of the seven strategies for success in a story/discussion/talk format, you are encouraged to fashion your own methodologies as to how to communicate these skills. If you decide to use the same story/discussion/talk method to teach your students as we present in this book, new and personalized stories can be offered that replace the ones in this book, making the "talk" much more personal and effective for the person "teaching" the strategies. Some teachers may even decide to present the message in a totally different format, but the commonality to this entire message is that students must be taught these strategies.

Students do not learn these strategies through osmosis alone. We have found if students are not taught these strategies, they will most likely never learn them on their own. Lastly, we believe the key to an administrator's or teacher's enjoyment of his or her job is directly tied to the ability to reach all students in profoundly positive ways. When teachers and administrators feel they are teaching students both cognitive skills and strategies that promote positive aspects of the affective domain, they become more fulfilled as educators (Harris, 2005).

The strategies are simple to understand and allow any person to easily apply the advice. When a student makes the decision to start using the advice in this book, immediate rewards and benefits will ensue. The more troubled the student, the more profound the change. But every student from the high achieving to the low achieving can benefit equally from this enlightening work of advice. Even adults will find the strategies enlightening to their own personal and professional lives. They work universally.

THE SUCCESS PILL

Education is the key to success.

—Jaime Escalante

We use the analogy of a *success pill* to illustrate a simple point. Imagine if someone invented a harmless pill that would ensure the person taking the pill lifelong success and happiness; everyone would quickly get the proper dosage. Everyone wants to be successful and happy. Those who claim they do not want happiness and success are merely stating the opposite for effect or to get much-needed attention. During our combined 40-year professional careers, we have never encountered a single student who did not want to be successful or happy, despite what the students portrayed. It is an innate need in all of us to be a success and to be accepted. We could call this imaginary pharmaceutical product the success pill.

As we all know, this is too good to be true. There is not, and never will be, a success pill, but the philosophies and advice espoused in this book are the success pill in the literary form. Read the book (swallow the pill), practice what this book espouses, and those same results will await you. The answer to motivating students is not some thing we do to them but rather arming them with the powerful strategies that they can easily implement to transform themselves in profoundly positive ways.

When we ask students privately and without peer influence if they want to be successful and happy, they invariably say, "Of course!" However, with some students, like Joe in the story in our introduction, who are struggling with life in general, saying yes to the above question seems like an unreachable goal or aspiration. Teachers should be aware that students will often act out negatively when confronted with a question of this type. It is best to simply accept the fact that all students want to know the secret to success and then proceed to motivate them to want to learn the secrets involved in the seven strategies. The change in motivation happens as the student becomes motivationally enlightened to the secrets of becoming successful in school and in life. Positive character traits and positive attitudinal changes follow as a result of this transformation.

Why do students and people in general continue to act in ways that will ensure their unhappiness or unsuccessful future? The answer is that people are humans; they have emotions; they have drive; they seek out adventure; they seek attention; they seek out their psychological and physical needs; they want to be noticed and accepted. All of these traits separate us from other classifications of higher-order animals. Even though our genetic compositions are 99.9% the same in all humans, this one tenth of a percent difference is what makes us all unique. This 0.1% difference is why there will always be students who are unmotivated and more likely to become societal failures. We truly believe all students can be reached if the administrator or teacher uses the skills necessary to reach them.

Reality demonstrates, however, that only a few people actually work hard enough to change themselves in the 6- to 8-week period it takes to make meaningful psychological change in their behaviors. Just like changing any bad habit or in creating new positive habits, a certain amount of time of sustained behavioral change is required to manifest the desired results. That effort is required in implementing the behavioral attitudes delineated in this book. We advocate patience and persistence in reaching those students that are hardest to change. You must stay the course and continually think about how to build strong relationships with those most at risk of educational and societal failure.

THE FAILURE MODEL

Failure is only the opportunity to begin again more intelligently.

—Henry Ford

We often use the *failure model* with students because it makes clear to them the potential wrong, unethical, immoral, or illegal direction their lives are taking. This failure model, if articulated properly, will have evidentiary effects on the person in which it is being used.

To begin discussion of the failure model, ask a student to list all the behaviors or traits required for a person to be successful and happy. Most likely, the students will list items like working hard, having a great attitude, being nice, abiding by the law, helping others, not doing drugs, refraining from sexual relations at too young an age, and so forth. Rarely will anyone list a physical trait such as being beautiful or smart. If they do, it will usually be only one physical trait and this can easily be explained away by giving examples of successful people. It is rare that a successful person is truly successful solely because of his or her physical beauty or academic intellect. These physical traits are largely genetic and, for the most part, cannot be changed. It is rare for such a trait, alone, to make a person successful.

Nearly all of the behavioral traits a student will list are attitudinal in nature. Thus, any student or person can choose to change existing behaviors or adopt the proper behaviors necessary to achieve success in all fashions of his or her life. The point to emphasize here is that all the listed traits leading to success can be accomplished by just about anyone. It is all about attitude and motivation—items one can control (Smink & Schargel, 2004).

Once the student finishes the first success model list, the student or class doing the exercise should brainstorm behaviors or actions that would guarantee a person would become a failure. This is the failure model. Students will generally list items like using drugs, lying, cheating, being untrustworthy, drinking, smoking, not coming to school, not studying, having a bad attitude, having premarital sex, breaking the law, and getting in trouble at school. Rarely will a student say that being "ugly" or being "dumb" has any impact on being a failure. This is important for those of us who work with students because it takes the excuses away from kids. The negative failure traits listed are almost always ones that anyone can avoid. It is largely a measure of choice and attitude on the part of the person to choose how to think and behave. Good thinking leads to good behaviors and positive habits.

The failure model is then used to show students that anyone can possess the abilities and traits necessary for failure or for success. The choice is just that—a conscious choice of positive behavioral actions. Once we have pointed out what causes *failure* or *success*, the foundation of understanding is in place for kids to build a structurally sound house in which to live their lives.

With the use of this model, many students will become aware of the critical choices that need to be made in life, school, and home. Students crave and yearn for guidance and leadership as they struggle to make sense of their lives. Through use of the failure model students begin to understand that much of what they are doing in school and in life is leading them to despair and misery. Through this understanding, students begin to ride the road toward the acquisition and development of positive character traits and successful life choices.

2

STRATEGY 1: THE POWER OF
MAKING CRITICAL DISTINCTIONS

For the strategies to truly be successful, five necessary concepts must be explained to students for them to fully understand and implement the strategies. Once these distinctions are made and the students completely understand them, they will usually find their attitude toward several situations will change.

These critical distinctions will help the students to see themselves in a different light—a light that shows potential for positive change. They are: maturity versus immaturity, ignorance versus stupidity, listening versus hearing, discipline versus punishment, and tattling versus being a good citizen. All five of these concepts comprise the first powerful strategy and will set the foundation for the remaining six powerful strategies.

MATURITY VERSUS IMMATURITY

Maturity consists of no longer being taken in by oneself.

—Chinese proverb

Before we begin teaching the seven strategies for success, we find it helpful to review with our students the clarification of how the word *maturity* is defined. At first, students may stretch and yawn thinking, "Here we go again; an adult telling us how to behave properly." After we define maturity in simplistic, easy-to-understand terms, the students will usually beam with acceptance of the explanation. They relate to and enjoy our definition of maturity because it frees them from the guilt of acting young, jocose, and frivolous at times; it also describes times when one must be serious.

We begin by telling stories of our own behaviors when others have erroneously labeled us or our actions as immature. Students like this analogy because it places us in the same dilemma that students have often experienced. We discuss how a professional might tease a colleague or family member, play practical jokes on people (we give specific examples), or act silly around our friends. None of these actions or any like them adequately rises to the level of immaturity. Immaturity is not defined by actions, but rather by situations. Any act done at an inappropriate time could be called immature and, likewise, any act done at an appropriate time and place can be considered mature. The difference is the situation and place in which the behavior is taking place.

For example, one does not laugh or "goof off" at a funeral. One does not feign accosting someone in a dark alley. One should not run when walking is required; one should not make noise when quiet is expected; one does not "horse around" when seriousness is the standard; and one does not talk out when silence is anticipated. Simply put, maturity is understanding the difference between when to be serious and when to have fun. Immaturity is failing to understand when it is appropriate to be serious and when it is appropriate to have fun. Students are rarely taught this simple concept. This explains why so many young adults are labeled as immature. When the students are given this definition along with several examples for clarification, they will grasp the important difference in the two terms. This distinction is critical for the success of both the students and the teachers and administrators.

The definition of maturity is often followed with an appeal to the students, letting them know that the information that will be shared will have a tone of seriousness; hence, maturity is expected of the student audience. Students have always accepted our challenge to be mature while we are giving the seven strategies for a successful life talk. Despite this challenge, the students are encouraged to laugh at the stories presented; in essence, the students should enjoy the talk. The message is far too important for anything less.

IGNORANCE VERSUS STUPIDITY

> Nothing in all the world is more dangerous than sincere ignorance and conscientious stupidity.
>
> —Martin Luther King Jr.

Another important clarification for students to understand is the difference between situations when people are labeled ignorant versus situations when people may be labeled stupid. The difference in these two seemingly derogatory terms refer to the actions and behaviors people choose based on a particular situation.

Ignorance is not necessarily a bad label, but stupidity almost always is a negative label for good reason. Many people inaccurately interchange the two terms or misuse the terms in their proper definitions. For purposes of clarifying these two terms, relative to our seven strategies for success, we define the terms as follows: *Ignorance* is simply acting without knowledge or knowing. This might include speeding when one is not aware of a certain speed limit or making cookies from a recipe that has an ingredient missing.

In both cases, one might say one is ignorant of the speed limit or ignorant of the ingredient left out of the recipe. If a car runs a stop sign when that driver has the right of way and a person is hit, then one can reasonably say that that person was ignorant of the fact that someone was going to run the stop sign. If one were to walk outside and be unfortunate enough to be struck by a small meteor, that person would be considered ignorant of the impending danger. If you made chocolate chip cookies from a recipe calling for 2 cups of flour, as opposed to 3 cups, you would be considered ignorant of the need to change. The list is infinite with regard to situations where using the term ignorant is appropriate.

Stupidity, on the other hand, refers to having knowledge of a particular situation, and then purposely choosing to ignore this knowledge. As a result, oftentimes an individual or group will act in ways that might endanger, negatively affect, or negatively impact the person acting or behaving in this manner. For example, a person speeding in a car knowing the speed limit, knowing a police officer is located over the next hill, yet choosing to ignore this knowledge; a person ignoring a stop sign on a small country road with corn growing high, obstructing the view of cross traffic; or innocent people venturing outside their homes ignoring the five o'clock news regarding meteor fragments falling from the sky.

Hundreds of examples of stupid actions and behaviors could be added to this list, but these few examples serve to better define the difference between the terms *stupid* and *ignorant*. Defining these two terms is critical in the search for positive behavior. Students have to be taught that many of their actions and behaviors are simply stupid and then encouraged to make changes in their behaviors for their own good. We then refer to this newly discovered knowledge on the part of students to admonish them to listen carefully because after the seven strategies are given and taught to the students, there no longer exists an excuse not to fully implement the newly discovered strategies.

When the teaching of the seven strategies for success is complete, a student can no longer plead ignorance to not knowing how to be successful in school and in life; the student now possesses all the knowledge necessary to change his or her life in profoundly positive ways. If the student then chooses to ignore the information professed during the talk or in this book, he or she could then be accurately labeled stupid. The word stupid usually offends students, so they are subtly being pushed to do the right things and for the right reasons. Students understand this concept easily and often portray their understanding after they are clarified in the talk.

To illustrate the point further, a story of an adventurous boy is told. This young boy made the trip to his best friend's house nearly every day, retracing his tracks day after day. As a result, no particular day stood out, until one day a bird unleashed a mess on his shoulder. As the little boy looked up at the flock of birds that was passing above he thought, if I had only known that the bird would poop on me, I would not have left the house until the bird had flown over the street. Although a harmless story, the little boy was experiencing the word ignorant in his own unique way.

The same boy, years later, could be seen incessantly teasing his neighbor's German shepherd so long as the animal was safely fenced in its backyard. The canine lived in the house most of the time but often slept on the back porch (out of view) when it was warm outside. The boy knew the dog could be lurking, ready to pounce and bite; yet the young boy decided to jump the fence to take a short route to the store. It seemed the risk was worth taking.

No sooner had the boy leaped the fence and started his sprint to the other side of the backyard when the dog sensed the presence of a predator. The dog dove from the porch and caught the boy and took a large section of his pants and small section of his buttocks before the boy was able to jump to safety over the fence. As he sprang to his feet, he said to himself, "Now that was stupid, I could have been mauled." The boy had unknowingly framed in his own mind the difference in the two terms. Unfortunately, most students do not develop this distinction on their own. This is why it is incredibly significant for us to help students make the distinction.

LISTENING VERSUS HEARING

> If we were supposed to talk more than we listen, we would have been born with two mouths and one ear.
>
> —Mark Twain

The third critical distinction students must learn is grasping the difference between listening to a message for understanding versus merely hearing the words without any meaningful learning occurring. When the teaching of the seven strategies for success begins, the administrator or teacher must make the distinction between these two words. Without this proper understanding, the students may never be in a position to fully grasp the meaning behind an adult's guidance. The students understand the difference between *hearing* (watching lips, experiencing a person say words without meaning, hearing "sounds," and so forth) and *listening* (understanding the message behind and ingrained in the talk). With this quick distinction made, most students come to realize the importance of this integral difference and choose to *listen* to the message, stories, and moral values coming from this important talk.

Listening requires a cooperative relationship between two participants interacting in dialogue; listening requires a compromising feel; and listening requires a dual emotional participation or buy-in. Hearing, on the other hand, simply requires turning up or down the "volume" of one's ears. Hearing does not require eye contact, relationship building, or trust. It simply involves the process of hearing "noise" or sounds. When hearing, very little information arrives at the necessary brain storage area; this information, therefore, will most likely never be used by the person hearing the words. In other words, hearing alone typically involves missing the message.

The following is a simple reminder to most of us who grew up watching Charlie Brown and his friends: They would often attend school in between their many adventures. The creator, Charles Schultz, did a fantastic job of illustrating Charlie, Linus, Lucy, and the others hearing the teacher. If you will recall, the teacher's voice was never audible or even identifiable. The noise could be heard, although the content was indecipherable. Perhaps if the students in Charlie Brown's class would have listened to their teacher, the content and knowledge being given would have been much more interesting.

Students must understand the nuances and differences conveyed in these two distinctly different words. Students and adults alike often will hear words that are being said, but for myriad reasons, the words being heard do not translate into meaningful listening. When one merely hears, one does not listen, and one cannot learn. When one listens, one learns in profoundly positive ways. The key for students to understand is that they must be aware of these two terms and to take steps to ensure that when a good message is offered through words, they must concentrate on the message and reflect on the meaning of what is being shared.

If one is sidetracked, busy doing something else, talking to their peers, fidgeting with something, distracted, or otherwise put into a position where one cannot listen, then the message is lost and no growth can take place. This happens in the classroom, on the field (court) of play, in the home, and in schools. In point of fact, the problem with listening properly can be seen at almost any time and in almost any location. But for the purpose of this segment, we will convey the meaning in terms of schooling.

Quite often, teachers, administrators, and parents are put into a position where they must discipline a child for some indiscretion. As in most cases, the child only hears words and not the intent of the message conveyed in these words. Very rarely will this student truly listen to what is being said so that he or she might understand the reasoning behind the discipline and the subsequent growth that can result in properly meted out discipline. If the message of discipline is lost to words and not followed by understanding (listening properly), then the discipline will fail to achieve its desired result. On the other hand, when a child understands the reasons and the positive growth potential of discipline, he or she grows immeasurably.

If an individual is truly participating in the conversation or talk, listening will be the selected avenue of understanding. This avenue leads to long-term memory, better understanding, and an enthusiastic response to the person who is speaking.

THREATS AND PUNISHMENT VERSUS DISCIPLINE

> Discipline is the soul of an army. It makes small numbers formidable, procures success to the weak and esteem to all.
>
> —George Washington

The fourth critical distinction administrators and teachers must convey to students is the necessity to develop discipline in their lives. To achieve this understanding, three terms must be fully understood: threats, punishment, and discipline. These three words require complete understanding so that kids and adults can adequately assess how people are addressing them or treating them with regard to what will happen to them based on carrying out certain undesirable behaviors. Students respond better to adults when they understand the meaning and purpose of these three commonly used words. One term should always be used, the other two terms rarely used or eliminated completely.

The terms threat and punishment should never be used in schools or in families. Threats and punishment are largely negative terms. In fact, the terms could easily be taken out of our vocabulary if humans would learn proper, positive behavior. The third term, discipline, is a positive word that should be used freely and often to help students learn boundaries of accepted behavior (Rosen, 2005a).

Threats refer to actions carried out against another person or object because the act or behavior is not acceptable to the person doing the threatening. All threats have an inherent ingredient that may include bodily harm, illegal action, or harming another person by abusive words, negative deeds, or physical harm. Threats are done with malice and usually involve forethought. There is intent to do harm to someone or some object. It is usually addressed by saying, "If you do this, then I will retaliate with this action or this behavior," a blackmail of sorts.

Punishment is an act of power over another as a result of acting out of retribution or revenge based on some action of another. Punishment usually involves some kind of physical or psychological pain to the recipient. It is often arbitrary and usually does not involve a positive warning of consequences. Punishment is generally done *to* someone, not *for* someone. A person being punished is being punished simply for actions or behaviors perpetrated on others, usually authority figures. It can be characterized by latent or manifested anger. The punishment administered to another is usually done quickly and with negative results for learning.

Punishment, at its core, is a form of retribution for actions deemed inappropriate by an authority figure. Punishment is not meant to be a teaching tool but rather a negative tool of revenge. Kids being punished feel powerless to prevent the punishment from happening. They often will rebel against the authority performing the punishment and will seek out ways to retaliate or rebel. This further exacerbates the problem and accelerates the hatred and mistrust that punishment promotes.

It is very important for administrators and teachers to understand that when discipline is enforced, the student will often feel as though he or she has been punished for some behavior or negative action, when, in fact, the administrator and teacher were meting out a given disciplinary consequence. It is vital that the adult explain the difference and the positive intentions of discipline, otherwise, when the student internalizes the discipline within a lens of punishment, he or she will often act out in very destructive ways. This destructive behavior is usually directed at any adult associated with the school.

These students will, more times than not, repeatedly lash out at the school itself by vandalizing the school or objects within the school. Additionally, these same students, who previously have been good students, may begin to exhibit behaviors that are antisocial and self-destructive. This negative behavior is a student's seemingly only way to get back at adults who are perceived to have done some punishing act to the student. If the student can be taught to understand that discipline is positive and directed toward helping him or her become a better person, the insightfulness of understanding can follow. If discipline is done with love and understanding, then the student will more readily accept the consequences of his or her actions. The next time a student is faced with a similar decision, the student may well refrain from making the same mistake twice (Orange, 2004).

Discipline is a concept all educators and parents should practice when teaching students proper boundaries and behaviors. Discipline comes from the word *disciple*, which means to teach or teacher. Therefore, when using disciplinary techniques and procedures, we are teaching kids proper behavior and boundaries. Consequences of behavior are clearly defined and articulated. Kids who ignore the consequences and receive discipline do so knowing they have the power to change their behavior and avoid the discipline.

Discipline is positive, clean, logical, natural, and consistent. It also allows for the perpetrator to take full responsibility for his or her actions. When discipline is explained and used properly, positive growth should follow. The control of behavior comes from within the behaving individual and not from the person doing the discipline. There is growth and power in discipline.

Discipline breeds improvement and allows the one who has misbehaved to take action in the future, hopefully to avoid discipline. Discipline, when administered properly, is good for the individual and for society in general. It takes invested time and patience to improve people's behavior, and discipline contributes in positive ways to this behavioral improvement. Once again, discipline is something a teacher or administrator does *for* a child and not *to* a child.

Explaining the differences among these three terms allows students to understand why schools and parents act the way they do when helping students. Schools and parents should never punish or threaten kids;

they should, however, discipline, when appropriate, with a clear conscience. Adults must teach the nuances of discipline to children of all ages. When discipline is used, students quickly understand the adults are trying to help them grow into productive, successful, and happy adults. This cannot be done using threatening or punitive techniques.

Students are more accepting of discipline because the consequences are spelled out in detail. The consequences make sense and are productive in their purpose. If a child knows that he or she will be grounded for 2 weeks for coming home 2 hours late and then chooses that behavior, he or she must be willing to take the consequential discipline. Discipline allows students to make conscious choices and moral decisions.

Students have control over what happens to them concerning discipline. Most kids understand and accept this type of consequence. They may not like the consequences of a particular action, but they understand and accept the outcome. Most students do not readily understand or accept punishment. If a child comes home 2 hours late and does not know there will be a consequence for his or her tardiness, then any action taken by the parents has the danger of becoming punishment. If the father grabs the car keys, grounds the child, and takes his or her weekend privileges away, then those actions may be justified on the part of the father.

However, without a child knowing the consequences and the parents articulating the resulting fallout, the child will not as readily accept the consequences, and the consequences are relegated to punishment. It is not what the discipline meted out is, but rather a conscious effort to give the child choices with his or her actions and not merely reacting to choices. This is another case of a person using proactive thoughts to prevent discipline versus reactive punishment for breaking some rule. Teaching disciplinary procedures is the answer to growing productive, successful children (Danforth & Smith, 2004).

During our seven strategies for success teaching/discussion/talk, students begin to accept our intentions better after we explain the differences in these three terms. These differences must be adequately understood before moving on to the next segment of the talk. We see an enlightened look on the faces of students who hear these definitions explained. The proverbial "light bulb" comes on and the change in knowledge can be seen on nearly every child's face. After learning this important distinction, students are now ready to hear about good citizenry versus "tattling" (snitching).

TATTLING VERSUS BEING A GOOD CITIZEN

No man is an island, entire of itself; every man is a piece of continent, a part of the main . . . any man's death diminishes me, because I am involved in mankind; and therefore never send to know for whom the bell tolls; it tolls for thee.

—John Donne

Teaching the concept of tattling versus being a good citizen can be very difficult for teachers and administrators of younger students in schools. Teaching positive character traits on how to be a good citizen may require counseling sessions with students when specific instances arise that may facilitate teaching the students about the power of being a good citizen versus just being a tattle. Teachers should enlist the help of parents and possibly community members to teach this important character trait.

The fifth critical distinction students must grasp to develop the social wherewithal necessary to become contributing citizens is understanding what being a good citizen means and how this differs from merely telling on someone. We have found students are particularly reticent about giving information concerning certain behaviors exhibited by others. Students often feel if they give information about something negative that has happened around school, they are "tattling" on their fellow classmates. Students often feel that if students perceive them as snitches, their peer group will ostracize, shun, or retaliate against them. This paralyzing dilemma prevents students from acting responsibly, as good citizens should act.

Other slang terms besides tattling may be used to describe telling on someone for some action: ratting out a classmate (a rat), snitching on a fellow student (a snitch), being untrustworthy, or not in the fold. This list is not all-inclusive, but does serve to give examples of slang terms students commonly use to describe this behavior. All of these terms or phrases are synonymous.

For point of clarification, students need to be taught that tattling is not productive, just like snitching can be counterproductive. These actions are bad for relationships because the terms imply telling on someone just to get that person in trouble with an authority figure. Telling on someone for the sole purpose of getting the individual in trouble is the wrong reason for divulging information about an incident.

When children are young, they quickly learn that if they tell on their brother or sister, just to get their way or to get them in trouble, they feel terrible inside. Children often tell for the wrong reasons when they are young. For example, a child may scream that Johnny just hit me or Johnny took my toy or Johnny spit on the sidewalk. This is tattling or snitching. It is used solely to get someone in trouble, and it is used many times to elevate the person telling to new and improved status.

Tattling also is a natural way for young children to develop a social conscience and decision-making ideals. Therefore, at a young age, these tattling and snitching episodes are natural, universal, and historical. Once a child becomes older, the tattling and snitching usually stops simply because of maturity. When discussing this subject with students it is imperative for them to understand the difference between good and bad telling. Once they discover the distinct difference between tattling and being a good citizen, they are free to make good decisions about divulging information. This, in turn, builds powerfully strong and positive character traits that will inevitably aid the student both in school and in life.

Being a good citizen involves protecting the school, home, neighborhood, shopping center, and so forth from people who exhibit behaviors that are threatening and intimidating to our general welfare. For example, if a student sees a drug deal going down or other students smoking marijuana on school property, it is his or her duty, as a school citizen, to report this information confidentially to the school authorities. This action protects the entire student body from possible harm. No one can argue that point.

If a student witnesses someone steal an item from a locker, he or she should report it. This is never tattling or snitching but rather being a good school citizen. When students have the urge to disagree about their civic duty, I give them the following example: If you were to witness someone breaking into your neighbor's home, would you let the burglars steal and plunder or would you call the police? If your own home were being burglarized and your neighbor witnessed it, would you want them to give you and the police the information? Of course you would! This illustrates the need for all students to become good citizens in the classrooms, on the athletic fields, in the performing arts arena, and at home. If students change their collective attitudes about good citizenry, the social benefit would be profound.

Unfortunately, students get confused about their civic duties, especially when those being accused may be their peers. They usually do not have the same conflict when reporting on people outside their social or peer group. This is an interesting phenomenon that needs to be addressed by adults. We would hope those educators reading this book would appreciate this significant phenomenon of how students must be taught the nuances of becoming a good citizen.

Students must be taught about their rights and obligations, beyond their own perceived world. Students have a larger civic duty to their schools, homes, jobs, families, and recreation areas. Most students lack this simple understanding of their role in society/school/home; it must be discussed and taught to them. This will enlighten the student and will lead to more productive relationships with others.

DEFINITION OF A FRIEND

Friendship without self-interest is one of the rare and beautiful things of life.

—James Francis Byrnes

The sixth and final critical distinction shared with students is the topic of what constitutes a real friend. Students mistakenly believe a friend is someone they hang out with, do activities with, and confide in on a regular basis. This is what we define as peer friendships. We prefer to call these peer relationships or peer associations. True friendship transcends these simple definitions of friendship. Students often feel as if their parents, teachers, administrators, and adult acquaintances were the "enemy." Students often perceive this because adult figures place restrictions on them, which might limit their freedom and choices. Adults know these restrictions and implementation of consequences are necessary to set proper boundaries for students as they mature into young adults. Without these defining guidelines in students' lives, they often will test limits far beyond that which is healthy. Students' peer friends are often their worst enemy by encouraging bad or illegal behaviors, harmful actions, and destructive tendencies. How can a student consider these negative influences as friendship?

With this question and the fundamental difference being hard to understand, this very occurrence is alive and flourishing with the youth of America. Of course, students need peer friendships, but students must be educated about the realities of peer friendship and the potential downfall of such relationships. If students would confide more in their teachers, parents, and adult relatives or acquaintances, their welfare would be greatly enhanced and their development would be more positive. It is rare that a peer friend has the wherewithal to give truly excellent advice. We always try to clarify and define the composition of true friendship. True friendship involves four identifiable characteristics:

1. A friend accepts one unconditionally.
2. A friend helps another to reach his or her full potential. They will do things and encourage activities that lead to one's success without jealousy or self-promotion.
3. A friend is someone one can confide in and trust completely. A friend will not pass judgment, but simply offer themselves as a listener and confidant. Advice that is offered from a true friend will always be in one's best interest.
4. A friend encourages proper behaviors, thoughts, and actions.

Many times a student will believe a peer is giving heartfelt advice, only to discover the advice/confidence shared was deliberately dreadful, encouraged unfortunate actions, or was shared with others. Through this series of misplaced trusts, a student will begin to understand who their true friends really are. This is where a trusted adult can help a student understand that most administrators and teachers have the best interest of the student at heart and will almost always give great advice to the student. Students must learn to understand that their previous definition of a friend must be completely reevaluated. Administrators and teachers can be real friends—professional, not personal. There is a huge differ-ence and educators must help students understand this difference. The results can be miraculous.

Students should be encouraged to understand that building profes-sional relationships with adults is healthy and good for their well-being. Students can become friendly with adults without becoming involved in more personal ways. We like to encourage students to get to know their parents and teachers personally without being personal.

Nearly all unhappiness stems from relationship problems with the people in our lives. When others betray students whom they believed to be their friends, students can recoil in fear and push everyone away, even the important adults in their lives. Working on building positive re-lationships will do wonders for students' psychological development. These relationships should extend to the adults in a student's life. We define these positive behaviors with adults or peers as rapport building or professional friendships. This topic will be discussed in later chapters.

True friendship involves developing relationships that are mutually productive and beneficial. Students must learn that friendship must be defined differently than it has been defined in the past. Once students understand this phenomenon, they are free to develop these friendship relationships to their personal benefit with adults and with their peer group (Roffey, 2004).

Once the critical distinctions are defined and discussed with students, they have a concrete foundation to better understand the seven strate-gies for success. Now the students are in a frame of mind to hear the next six powerful strategies that will lead them to success in school and in life, effectively motivating the unmotivated.

SUMMARY

These six critical distinctions need to be addressed and discussed with students to build a solid foundation of understanding before students can effectively digest the positive information promoted in this book. This chapter is critical for students in their overall understanding of the purpose of the seven strategies for success. This first powerful strategy lays the foundation for the next six strategies.

This book is a creative prescription conceived to fulfill a need to help kids succeed in school and in life. This book is a true motivational experience, not only for students, but also for those adults involved in the students' lives. It is an enlightening message that we discovered in our quest to become great teachers and administrators. As beginning teachers and fledgling administrators, we needed to develop strategies that would help students to succeed and to change the behaviors that can almost ensure failure. That is how this book and the messages it espouses were born. Through these messages and strategies, almost all of the students we have encountered throughout the years have implemented these powerful strategies and have changed portions of their lives, attitudes, behaviors, and relationships to better themselves. This is what this book is truly about—the motivation of students to take on positive behaviors.

This chapter simply sets the foundation of understanding. The next few chapters will take each of the remaining six strategies, describe it, discuss it, and give varying examples and stories of how to properly implement it for a profoundly positive and successful life. The student who grasps the power of these suggestions will motivate him- or herself. No one will have to do it for them. Making this change will be a conscious decision—one born of want and need.

❸

STRATEGY 2: THE POWER OF BUILDING STRONG AND RESILIENT RELATIONSHIPS

Some people come into our lives and quickly go. Some stay for awhile and leave footprints on our heart, and we are never, ever the same.

—Anonymous

Numerous books and articles have been written on the subject of building relationships, both personal and professional. In the references section of this book you can read example after example of the importance of relationship building as the very core of nearly all teaching and disciplinary effectiveness. Therefore, you should be aware that this chapter is not intended to duplicate the wealth of knowledge the public has learned on this critical subject, but rather it should be used to point out a few new ideas we have found that have been particularly effective with building character and promoting success in a student's development (Kaplan, 2004).

We want to point out some obvious nuances of building relationships and offer some insights into some not-so-obvious reflections on how administrators and teachers can build highly productive relationships with students. Some of the suggestions given here can be found in many sources, but they are not credited to any one source but rather are universally applicable to all people. No author has ownership in these strategies to build strong, interpersonal relationships.

You must understand that the world we now live in is much different from that of several decades ago. Educators must be sensitive to touching, to making personal remarks aimed at physical attributes, to being alone with students in certain situations, and to be sensitive to individual differences that may offend one student but not another. We advocate getting to know the students personally without being personal. You should reflect for a moment on that statement before reading further.

Although suggestions will be given to build strong and powerful relationships, one must never forget the professional distance an educator must keep with students. Having said those words, it is imperative that educators not allow this fear to keep them from developing strong and resilient relationships that can have a profoundly positive influence on students.

Students come to school from varying backgrounds. Some come to school happy, others sad, others angry, others enthusiastic. Some are highly intelligent, while others struggle to learn. Some are loved unconditionally at home, while others are trying to find the love that is missing at home. Some students do not readily trust and cannot be trusted; others are highly honest and trustworthy. Simply put, every child is unique and he or she comes to school with highly individualistic needs and wants. We believe every child craves acceptance and professional love from his or her teacher.

Children yearn to have adults in their lives that sincerely care about their well-being. All students crave this caring attitude and nearly all students will respond to adults that exhibit a caring attitude. When a professional educator supplies this innate need, unbelievable progress can be made in motivating students.

A historical story concerning the importance of developing and nurturing relationships involves two noteworthy individuals. A poor Scottish farmer named Fleming was farming his land. While churning the land and planting seeds, he heard a cry for help coming from a nearby swamp or bog. Fleming quickly dropped his tools and ran to the bog. There, mired to his waist in mud and muck, was a terrified young boy, screaming and struggling to free himself. Farmer Fleming saved the young lad from what could have been a slow and terrifying death. The next day, a fancy, royally adorned carriage pulled up to the Scottish farmer's sparse surroundings. An elegantly dressed nobleman stepped out and introduced himself as the father of the boy farmer Fleming had pulled from the mud and muck. The nobleman insisted on repaying the farmer for saving his son's life. The farmer would not accept payment, consistently waving off the continuous offers.

At that moment, the farmer's own son came to the door of the family hovel. The nobleman asked, "Is this your own son?" The farmer replied proudly that it was. Upon this knowledge, the nobleman made a deal with the farmer. He would provide the farmer's son with the same level of education his own son would enjoy. Farmer Fleming agreed to this joyous offer and the young son attended the very best schools. In time, the farmer's son graduated from St. Mary's Hospital Medical School in London, England, as the noted Sir Alexander Fleming, the discoverer of penicillin. Years afterward, the same nobleman's son who had been saved from the bog by farmer Fleming was stricken with pneumonia. What saved his life this time? Penicillin. The name of the nobleman was Lord Randolph Churchill; the name of the nobleman's son was Sir Winston Churchill.

We believe the foundation of all learning is the mutually strong relationship between the teacher/administrator or parent and the child. If a negative relationship is evident between student and parent/teacher, the student will often defy this person and will refuse to cooperate, let alone learn or accept consequences. These students can disrupt the entire learning environment. A defiant child can often disrupt the entire family core. Therefore, the single best way to reach a student is to build a strong, interpersonal, and professional relationship with the student.

The following is a list of ways and methodologies that work in building, fostering, retaining, and making resilient relationships between student and teacher. Learning these relationship-building skills will simultaneously develop positive character traits in these students as well because the students will see a positive role model exhibiting positive interpersonal relationships skills. Please remember the following when developing professional relationships with students:

- Never single a student out in front of his or her peers for any kind of discipline, regardless of how tempting it may be in the heat of the moment.

- Never single a student out in front of his or her peers for public recognition. Yes, you read it right. Many people mistakenly think it is appropriate to single people out for praise in front of their peers. This thinking is a hackneyed approach to giving praise and is often ephemeral in results at best. These behaviors can often be counterproductive to what is actually intended. (*This is not inconsistent with what has been mentioned earlier, but rather a specific example of demonstrating the potential shortfalls of singling individuals out for positive comments in front of their peers.*) Please read on.
- Say hi and goodbye to every student but particularly the unmotivated. Do this every single time you see a student entering the school or your classroom and every time you see them leave the classroom or building. Do this every single day—do not miss a day! The students will notice.
- Always smile when you see the student unless you are disciplining the student for some infraction of the rules. In this case a serious, no nonsense approach is vital.
- Whenever possible, do something nice for the student. Steven Covey calls these "putting deposits into people's emotional bank accounts" (Covey, 1998). Then when a teacher or administrator needs to make a withdrawal (a request for some desired behavior), there is "money" in his or her account that can be withdrawn. If one never puts in a deposit, how can one make a withdrawal? Although Covey puts it this way, the concept is universal. Simply put, be service oriented to the student. Shepherd them in the right direction by doing good deeds for them whenever possible. This not only models good behavior but demonstrates to students that we are willing to go out of our way to help them and care for them.
- Tell students you are always there for them to help in any avenue they desire—schoolwork, problems, advice, and so forth. In addition to communicating this important fact, it is critical that the teacher/administrator follow through with this concept.
- An occasional pat on the back works well to demonstrate caring. (See our earlier concerns on touching.)
- Write personal notes that are not personal in nature. For example:
  —You did a great job on the quiz.
  —You hustled in the game last night.
  —I appreciate your effort on this project.

—You are getting smarter by the day, I can see it.
—Thank you for working so hard in my class.

The items mentioned above should never be done in front of peers and only on occasion. Never say anything of a personal nature like:

- You have beautiful hair.
- You have the most gorgeous brown eyes.
- You are a hunk.
- If I were 16 again, I'd hit on you.

As silly as this may seem, some teachers make this mistake, which can have devastating consequences. Be sure to keep the comments on the professional side except in cases when you want to show genuine caring. Ideas of this nature are great and may not seem out of the ordinary in speaking or writing to some of our brightest and best-behaved students, but educators tend to ignore the unmotivated in dealing with the same issues. The student will respond like one has never seen them respond to these types of methods. Once again, these acts should be done in private and not in front of the peer group.

- Shake hands when you see them out of the building and in a situation where they are by themselves or with a friend or with parents. Shaking hands is a powerful way to build strong relationships that is largely ignored.
- Wave to students when you see them out in public and give them a big smile. If they come up to you after that, shake hands as mentioned earlier and enjoy a casual conversation.
- Attend extra curricular events and then comment about the event when you see the student the next time.
- Learn who the parents are and talk to them if you see them at an event or at school. Many students do not have visible parents, but some have parents who do attend events. Either way, seek them out and have conversations with them—the same goes for brothers and sisters. Make the connection with siblings, regardless of how different the sibling may be from the brother or sister in your classroom.
- Be pleasant and friendly in the hallways, cafeteria, gymnasium, and before and after school when you see students gathering.

- Don't be afraid to walk down the hall talking to a student—particularly the unmotivated.
- Ask students to come in before and after school to get help with their schooling or life in the classroom, particularly the student who rarely gets this opportunity.
- Show trust in students by giving them trusted duties in the classroom (watering plants, delivering items to the office, and so forth). Demonstrate trust in what you allow them to do. They will not let you down if you tell them you trust them to do certain chores you usually leave for more motivated students.
- Make only positive comments about students around other teachers. These comments always get back to the student and can perpetuate negative feelings about students.
- It is critical that you learn every student's first name very quickly—the last name is less important. The importance of knowing a student's first name is always underappreciated. Many teachers do not seem to understand the significance of this simple gesture. By learning the students' names, you have shown ownership and enthusiasm for all those in your room.
- Address students by their first name or nickname and never by their last name. Do not address students as Mr., Miss, or Ms. That is too formal and gives the impression of phoniness. It also shouts at the student as they try to figure why they are being addressed the way an adult is addressed. We also suggest learning the parents' first names and calling them by that first name and not Mr., Miss, or Ms. with their last name. It makes for a more friendly and open exchange regardless of the reasons or situations surrounding the meeting with the parents.
- Teachers and administrators must genuinely learn to be helpful to everyone, not just those they feel more comfortable helping. Students must learn everyone is equally important in a classroom or in a school—even the unmotivated must learn this. As the student begins to witness that the *right* way to treat people is to treat everyone equally well, they become aware of their place in the bigger scheme of things. Unfortunately, some students seek more attention by acting out in inappropriate ways. These are key to building strong and resilient relationships.

These suggestions can be used to build strong, positive, long-lasting, and resilient relationships with others. You will undoubtedly have additional ones to add to the list. It is imperative to reflect on this list and to formulate a list of ways to build these same kinds of relationships.

The noted psychologist and educator William Glasser (1998) is known for saying that all unhappiness revolves around relationship problems. To take this thought a bit further, we believe that without strong, positive, and resilient relationships, happiness will always be illusive. In order to be happy, one must develop these relationships. Humans are not wired to be isolated without the nurturing benefits of other humans. In the rare cases when isolation in humans is witnessed, that loneliness usually stems from some sort of abnormal mental condition. This is not to say that people do not, from time to time, seek to be alone, but when it becomes the normal state of affairs it is abnormal.

Humans love to belong to a group and to be accepted, so the student either outwardly or stealthily (subconsciously) wants to fit in and to be successful in life. We believe this is a fundamental need of all humans. One can extrapolate from these premises that if the student is not happy (and they almost always are), then there is an underlying relationship problem. It is also true that this relationship may be so traumatic and injurious that the student may not share the problem with anyone (Glasser, 1990).

Glasser (1998) also talks about students and their reluctance to let adults into their quality world. If a student builds a significantly strong relationship with an adult to allow that adult into his or her quality (inner) world, then the adult is in a very powerful position to encourage positive change in the child. We agree. To reach the student, teachers and administrators must work hard to build relationships with students that will allow the student to "let" the adult into his or her quality (inner) world. The bulleted list in this chapter will help the reader develop those insights into how to do just that.

TYPES OF MOTIVATIONS TO REMEMBER IN BUILDING RELATIONSHIPS

It can be assumed the reader of this book knows the three basic motivations in moving people to do a particular behavior or action. This segment of the chapter will not delve into these because it would be a redundant exercise considering previous authors have exhaustively explored this area. Any teacher or administrator is well aware of the shortcomings of each type of discipline. Simplified, these three types are as follows:

1. A type of reward is offered for some act or behavior to motivate the person.
2. A type of punishment or discipline is offered for some act or behavior to motivate a person to change that action or behavior.
3. The third type is supposed to work best—it is intrinsic motivation. In other words, figure out how to make children want to do it for their own intrinsic good. Goals are often cited as ways to do this (Tileston, 2005).

In addition to these three motivational techniques, we believe there is an overlooked fourth motivator, not available in the literature: Building strong relationships will motivate people to listen so that positive change can take place (Deiro, 2004; Reider, 2004; Whitaker, 2003). If a teacher can build a strong, positive, and resilient relationship with a student, he or she can motivate the unmotivated to change in profoundly positive ways. In short, a relationship can motivate a person to want to do something simply to please the person or not let them down. This is rarely mentioned by experts on motivation or in books or journals written on the subject. For example, a player playing for a particular coach may be devoted to the coach so much and have developed such a strong relationship with the coach that the player will do nearly anything the coach wants him or her to do. This is an extremely powerful tool to motivate people, but there can be risks.

- Adults must be cognizant of the fact that this power can also lead to negative influence (Winograd, 2005). Many examples can be given when an adult figure takes advantage of a relationship with children they supervise for selfish reasons. A teacher or coach who has an affair with an underage student or player is an example of this bad influence. A teacher who influences a student to do something the student should never be asked to do, such as giving the teacher extra food at a restaurant, not charging for something regularly bought in a store, stealing for the adult, doing drugs, sexual favors, and a number of other likewise unethical/immoral/illegal acts, is another example.

- To reach the student (indeed any student), the greatest single motivator is to build a strong, positive, and resilient relationship that motivates the student to want to be motivated to please the teacher or administrator just for the sake of pleasing the person and not wanting to let him or her down. In other words, you use the powerful influence you develop through relationships to get desired behaviors or actions.

- The last part in building these strong interpersonal relationships is moving the unmotivated beyond pleasing the adult to motivating the child to be successful beyond this relationship. To accomplish this goal and to prove ultimately successful with students, the gauge of success is measured by how well the unmotivated becomes motivated beyond the realm of the one strong relationship into all relationships. This is the goal in reaching the unmotivated and unsuccessful. Once the one interpersonal relationship is sufficiently strong, the influence can be exerted to affect change in total behavior in all areas of the child's life. It really is that simple.

Table 3.1 lists anachronistic ways we treated students compared with the new ways that must be implemented to motivate the unmotivated. In many classrooms, it has been demonstrated time and again that nearly every student can be motivated by building a strong foundation of relationship building. Therefore, the student invites the teacher or the administrator into their quality lives (Glasser, 1998) as a participator and empathizer. In addition to these academic relationships, we often witness a student building strong relationships with others outside the classroom (social peers, community members, parents, and so forth).

Once this invitation has taken place, a student will be motivated to please the teacher or administrator in profoundly positive ways. Once the foundation is in place the teacher or administrator can begin the

Table 3.1. Anachronistic Ways We Treated Students Compared With the New Ways That Must Be Implemented to Motivate the Unmotivated

Old Ways	New Ways
Ignore students	Seek out the unmotivated or unsuccessful
Confront students with anger	Never confront in anger
Confront students with threats	Discipline as the foundation
Allow failure (as an illustration to others)	Failure is not an option
Rationalize reasons for being unmotivated	No acceptance of excuses
Blame the student	Adult takes ownership in problem
Offer bribes for certain behaviors	Never bribe, use sarcasm, or belittle
Not helping students in need	Always willing to help
Ridicule in group settings	Never single out in front of peers
No respect for the student	Always respectful
No attempt at building rapport	Always building rapport
No attempt to build strong relationships	Build strong relationships
Not caring	Deep caring
Not loving	Build professional love for all
No empathy for problems/desire for immediate results with little patience	Total empathy
Accept acrimonious behavior	Get to the root of the problem
Make excuses for an unsuccessful class	No excuses, only changes
Remove the unmotivated	Insist on success in school
Be perfidious to students	Demonstrate loyalty to students
Pretentious front in the classroom	Genuineness in the classroom
Tenacity in a negative way	Tenacity in a positive way
Transient view of problems	Long-term solutions
Demand venerable respect	No age barriers to reaching students

enjoyment of watching the student become motivated. Motivation will take place if the strategies listed in this book are followed, but without this foundation of relationship building, the structure being built will not last. On the other hand, by building a strong foundation of relationships nearly any structure will result in success.

Teachers and administrators know now more than ever that it is not *what* we teach students that will make them successful people but *how* we teach them that is paramount. In today's world, the "what" is achieved for the educator with the present national standards movement. Standards are meaningless without students willing to learn and grow. As professional educators, building rapport with students, understanding and teaching to the uniqueness of individual students, and stressing the importance of students reaching their individual potential are the keys to what schooling should be about (Theobald, 2005).

This is not an all-inclusive guide to building enduring relationships. Other authors have devoted entire books to the subject of this chapter. The reason this chapter is a vital part of the seven strategies for success is because every researcher basically articulates the same thing—education is about people and relationship building. If this critical piece is missing, some students will never understand how to become a success in school and in life. As a result, positive character building will also suffer. Therefore, empower your students and model this critical strategy. Build relationships that last a lifetime!

4

STRATEGY 3: THE POWER OF
AVOIDING NEGATIVE ATTENTION

The power of choosing good and evil is within the reach of us all.

—Origen

When one examines the life of any successful person or person of character, one will almost always see common traits. Although success can be defined in any number of ways, we define success as a journey and not a destination. A successful person is one who may not be perfect, but rather one who aspires to that goal in all of his or her actions and deeds. Some adjectives are typical of successful people: service oriented, a giving rather than taking, hardworking, honest, trustworthy, ethical, moral, legal, ethical, and other similarly positive words. This chapter is devoted to teaching students how to build strong character by developing these very traits in their daily lives. By bringing positive attention to oneself, a person begins to see how perception of him- or herself (and others) will change.

By stressing to students that the collective good is sometimes more important than the individual good, they will come to understand the importance of citizenship. Giving to others and serving others are a large part of what is behind the strategy outlined in this chapter. As you begin to read this chapter in detail, you are encouraged to see how practicing these commonsense behaviors can subtly change character traits that those who are most successful exhibit.

George Nelson (2005) writes in his book *Breaking the Learning Barrier for At-Risk Students* that students (particularly the at-risk student) can many times learn much better in a nontraditional environment, that students learn better when learning is tied to emotions, and that all learning is value driven on the part of the individual student. Please pause to see how this concept fits into this chapter by understanding that it can be a challenge to engage all students in the learning environment.

Although most educators today are aware of what needs to be done in the classroom to engage students, the reality is that few teachers can do this on a day-to-day basis. This is where this chapter comes into play. It is better to try to shift students from a standpoint of "the world evolves around them" to a more worldly view, one in which they can become active. The latter viewpoint has more enduring and lasting effects, rather than a more personal and selfish trend.

Being successful in the classroom is critical to being successful in life. Therefore, we will devote much time to giving advice and stating strategies that create positive attitudes to help motivate students. Helping to change the attitudes of students by empowering them with knowledge is much more effective than changing teachers' strategies of conducting lessons within their classrooms. It has been our experience that once students become enlightened to what it takes to be successful using the seven strategies, it is a rare occurrence when the student does not begin to change behaviors and attitudes.

Nearly all students are capable of doing something that can be construed as being negative by a teacher or an adult figure. These negative actions and behaviors have the potential to destroy relationships between students and teachers. When the relationship is damaged, so too is the student's potential for success. Although students can survive the deterioration of rapport with a teacher, they stand to benefit from a culture-positive relationship. The advice to all students is to simply refrain from doing anything a teacher can construe as being negative.

This may seem incredibly simple, but it is actually profound in terms of a student's ability to build a relationship with the teacher; thus the student will develop a successful and positive relationship with that teacher.

We believe the first foundation block to building success is to develop positive relationships with teachers. Obviously, this should extend to parents, friends, acquaintances, and neighbors as well. However, for our purposes here, we will concentrate on the student-teacher relationship.

Students often believe they are "invisible." What kind of a statement is this? Please let us explain. Students know they are not transparent, but they often mistakenly believe their actions can go unnoticed or undernoticed because they are just one of many at any given time in any given circumstance. After all, if the teacher does not say anything, he or she must not see it happening; after all, if I show up late to work (along with several other of my fellow employees) the boss won't notice; after all, how can a teacher pick one student out of a large crowd of people?

Not only can teachers pick a student out of a crowd, they do it regularly, either incognito or directly. The fact is nearly every teacher witnesses, either directly or circuitously, actions or behaviors students undertake. Rarely does an action go unnoticed by a teacher. The teacher, however, may not call attention to every single negative happening. Rarely will a negative action go unnoticed in the other facets of the student's life. A student's boss will most likely notice late arrival time, poor organizational skills, or a lazy attitude toward chores or other actions on the job.

Students can be exposed to this simple mind-trap: because there are 25 to 30 students in their classroom, it must be impossible for a teacher to see them. How can a teacher see this many students at one time? Often students will sit in the back of the classroom, "hidden" behind those in front of them. A common fallacy of students is that if they "hide" behind someone, they cannot be seen writing notes, cheating on tests, picking their noses, throwing pencils, and so forth. Another mind-trap includes not looking at the teacher; after all, if the student does not look at the teacher when doing something, surely the teacher will not notice. All are fallacies and students must understand this reality. Few students truly understand the impact of bringing negative attention to themselves. Even fewer students truly understand the impact of bringing only positive attention to themselves everyday.

An exercise we use with students is the peripheral vision example. We model by placing both hands and arms out to our sides like we are getting ready to spread our "wings." Arms are 180 degrees opposite one another. We explain that while looking straight ahead we cannot see our fingers wiggling because they are outside our peripheral vision. As one brings the arms, fingers wiggling, slowly forward, the fingers will eventually be visible to the eyes. The pointing fingers from both hands will show the angle of vision that extends to the horizon. The best estimate of the actual angle is somewhere around 160 degrees.

This means that a teacher facing the front of a classroom can see every child within this same area, thus, the teacher can see any student within the scope of the peripheral vision. Any movement on the part of students can easily be seen if they are in the peripheral vision area. The students come to understand how easy it is for a teacher to see even the slightest movement.

We have personally witnessed kids picking at pimples, adjusting their underwear, cleaning their ears, combing hair, passing notes, giving obscene gestures, tapping pencils on the desktop, taking contacts in and out, putting on makeup, throwing trash on the floor, and any number of other distractive movements. Students must remember these occurrences seemingly convince the teacher the student is not listening, not paying attention, or preoccupied with something less important than what the teacher is teaching.

The following story illustrates this very point. Jim was a student in a sixth-grade art class. The first day of class Jim was seated in the last row of class. As class was prepared for what they needed for tomorrow, Jim was slouched down in his seat, hidden almost totally by the girl in front of him. As the talk continued, Jim was writing something on a sheet of paper. It quickly became clear that he was writing a note to someone.

Finally, he finished his writing and began to slowly fold the paper into a small square. He even made eye contact with the teacher several times while he folded the paper into a neat little triangle. The teacher waited patiently until the end of the period so as not to embarrass him in front of his peers.

When Jim approached the desk, the teacher asked him what was so important that he had to write in class. At first he acted incredulous but quickly changed his demeanor once he noted the teacher was not going to accept his denials. He asked, "How did you know?" The teacher acknowledged that it all would be explained to him tomorrow during the seven strategies for success talk.

All teachers remember their first day of teaching. Most of us approach the classroom with wide eyes and a fear in our minds. Very rarely do students understand the importance of first impressions. The following story helps to explain how one of us dealt with a classroom full of horrible first impressions.

I arrived at school by 6:30 A.M., had my copies made, my bulletin boards decorated, my desks organized, my board washed. When the bell rang, my heart began to race. Most students came into the room with a look of sure bewilderment. After all, I had mostly freshmen, who were approaching their first high school class. With this in mind, my confidence level rose. They, too, were scared and fearful of the unknown. However, when Gina walked into the room, the entire attitude changed.

Gina walked to the back of the room, sat on the countertop, and began to sing loudly. I had decided to allow this rude (and quite annoying) behavior to continue, up until the bell rang. The bell rang and the other 30 students made their way to their seats. Gina, on the other hand, was still sitting on the countertop. As I began my trek around the room, I slowly walked back to where Gina was located. I continued on with my reading of the classroom strategies and rules. While doing so, I quietly asked Gina to please remove herself from the counter.

The students were eagerly watching and waiting for Gina to erupt. The students knew Gina as a "bad student" who regularly tested teacher/student boundaries and rules. Suddenly, Gina let out a yelp, stating she had a "right" to sit on the counter. Now, the entire class was disrupted and all students were staring blankly at me, wondering what I would do next.

I asked again, more sternly, for Gina to remove herself, and she exclaimed she would not, under any circumstances, get off the counter. Despite my continual warnings and increasing volume, I decided to let her sit on the counter for the remaining minutes of the period. I would keep her after class. After all, I had the perfect solution to her ludicrous behavior—my talk on the seven strategies for success.

Students like Jim and Gina do any number of silly actions that bring negative attention to them. Teachers rarely see students for the first time and instantly form negative opinions about them unless they do something immediately to bring negative attention toward themselves. Teachers should not have preconceived notions about students; however, slowly and incrementally, the teacher sees every student's behavior and actions and these eventually lead to the formation of an opinion about specific students.

As the days go by, these actions, if perceived to be negative, build up in the teacher's memory to the point where an opinion, however fallible, is formed. If the forming opinion is negative, then the relationship is damaged, and thus the student's propensity for success has suffered a setback. Students must always be cognizant of this fact and do or say nothing that might be conceived as negative to the teacher. Here are a few common mistakes students make the first day and throughout the term. They include sayings or actions on the part of students. These statements are considered to bring negative attention to oneself and must be avoided.

- My brother/sister/mom/dad had you and she/he didn't like you.
- I heard you are a hard teacher.
- I heard your tests are impossible.
- I heard you are mean.
- Why do we have to take this class?
- Why do we have to have a seating chart?
- Why is this place like a prison?
- You make this impossible/you can't teach.
- Why are we taking a quiz?
- I failed this test because you didn't explain the material well enough.
- Why do we have to learn this stuff?
- This is dumb.
- I'm not doing this or that.
- I'll call or tell my mom or dad.
- I'm reporting you to the principal.
- I don't have to do this because my mom said I didn't have to.
- I hope I don't have you next year.

Likewise these actions produce negative impressions:

- Talking while the teacher is talking.
- Laughing out loud at inappropriate times.
- Making fun of people in class.

- Making fun of the teacher.
- Tardiness/truancy.
- Wanting to leave early/hurrying to be the first one out of class.
- Tearing up a test or quiz when the grade is not the best.
- Not keeping work, throwing it away immediately.
- Bragging.
- Nagging/complaining/criticizing.
- Horseplay/giggling when not appropriate.
- Hurting others.
- Being close-minded.
- Showing off in front of peers.
- Harassing other students.
- Cheating in any number of venues and ways.
- Not turning in homework.
- Doing work in a sloppy, haphazard way.
- Running inside the building.
- Slapping or tripping other students intentionally.
- Sleeping in class.
- Not paying attention to the teacher when he or she is talking.
- Combing hair, putting on make-up, or playing with their hair incessantly.

These lists are by no means complete, but most struggling students will see themselves in at least a few of the examples mentioned above. A student can survive one episode of any of these indiscretions, but when they happen time and again or become the norm, then the student is in jeopardy of not being successful in a given class or with a certain teacher. The following story illustrates another example of a student's negative behavior.

Rick was adept at being the center of attention. Rick believed he was the unofficial keeper of student exploitation. Rick routinely made snide remarks in class to make other students laugh. He also became the class's negative spokesperson whenever something was assigned that might meet with some resistance—assignments like quizzes, homework, outside projects, term papers, and so forth. He would routinely frown when the teacher was assigning work or would speak out at injustices he felt were being inflicted on other students. If he was bored, he would tap his pencil; if he was upset, he let someone know; if he did not get his way, he whined; and when he entered the room, it was a theatrical performance.

After Rick heard the seven strategies for success talk, the teacher waited to see how he reacted. Rick came in after school and talked to the teacher for over 40 minutes. It was unbelievable how Rick opened up. He said he really never understood how his teachers perceived his behaviors. Several students and teachers commented on how Rick had changed.

Unbelievably enough, Rick went on to become a star basketball player in college and is now the principal of a large suburban high school. Rick gives a similar seven strategies for success talk to his senior students each year. Rick not only practiced the seven strategies, but he, too, preached them to students who needed them the most.

Negative behavior can include cheating and other forms of dishonest behavior. Students who cheat always want to know where the teacher is located. They want to sit as far away from the teacher as possible. They will constantly look up to see if the "coast is clear." The cheater has formed an excuse and has practiced, methodically, how to discard the evidence, if need be.

Sandy was no exception. She was seated in a corner section of the room, facing the front of the room with her leg clearly visible to her eyes. Even though the teacher could not see the cheat sheet or see her eyes, he knew what she was doing after a few looks in her direction. The teacher did not mention the incident, nor did Sandy admit to her dishonesty.

Interestingly, she never looked at the teacher and avoided him whenever possible. Her actions were totally out of guilt because the teacher had never confronted her nor had the teacher ever suggested she had done anything wrong. Unfortunately, the relationship could have been mended had the teacher said something right away; the teacher could have helped her grow as a person and accept responsibility for her actions. After Sandy heard the strategies talk the next year, she returned to this teacher, stating her dishonesty, and requested to take the test again, under strict guidance.

Some students might ask why teachers don't understand that these negative words, actions, or behaviors do not necessarily reflect on the teacher or mean the student is a bad person. In other words, these negative actions or indiscretions are not always intended to be mean or to reflect a bad attitude. However, students need to understand that a negative impression is almost always what results from this type of behavior. This is why it is critical for the student to fully grasp the importance of avoiding negative attention.

Teachers are human, just like students. They have feelings and needs just like everyone else. It isn't that the teacher doesn't like the student; it simply means the teacher is filling his or her brain with negative garbage about the student. Once this garbage fills the brain, it is nearly impossible to remove it. It is possible to remove the garbage, but the smell may linger for a long time. The trick is to avoid negative actions, words, and indiscretions all of the time.

5

STRATEGY 4: THE POWER
OF POSITIVE BODY LANGUAGE

Do what you can, with what you have, wherever you are.

—Eleanor Roosevelt

The importance of avoiding negative behaviors and actions, which could (and probably would) create tension and turmoil between the student and the reciprocating person, has been discussed. This chapter explores another simple technique that has a profound effect on a teacher's attitude toward a student. When a student uses this technique occasionally and appropriately, the effects can be strikingly positive and will contribute to building a successful relationship with the teacher.

Although effective with teachers, this particular strategy is extremely effective with parents, friends, neighbors, acquaintances, and professionals alike. In addition to this little known powerful technique, there are other body language messages that can be equally effective. Teachers and administrators should become totally familiar with all of these body language messages and demonstrate to students how these subtle messages can send strong signals.

NODDING OF THE HEAD

The first seemingly magical technique is nodding one's head in an approval gesture. This is done at certain times, while someone is talking with or talking to another individual or group. As simple as this technique appears on the surface, it sends a powerfully, positive message to the person speaking. Here are a few powerful messages this technique sends. It tells the person:

- You enjoy his or her company;
- You are paying close attention;
- You agree with what the person is saying;
- You are intrigued by the information given;
- You want more information;
- You are eager to learn;
- You enjoy his or her class;
- He or she is interesting to listen to;
- You are on his or her side and an advocate for learning.

One might ask how someone nodding his or her head could possibly project these emotions. The reason is simple. We all want to be liked and accepted. It is a fundamental law of human nature. When someone agrees with us, which is what the nod does, it sends a message of acceptance. This, in turn, sends a powerful feeling of peer approval. This also has the potential to increase the individual's motivation, build positive rapport with the person, and start the process of respect building. To illustrate how powerful this simple technique can be, we tell two short anecdotes.

Carol was an average student who had just learned the seven strategies for success. She and her class of home economics students were invited to hear the governor speak at a midmorning gathering of a local women's group. Carol was seated with her teacher and fellow students near the back and middle of the group. Numerous schools attended, and the room was packed. As the governor began his speech, Carol turned her chair around to face the governor. She positioned herself so that she could clearly see his face, and so he would clearly see her's.

The moment she turned her chair, he glanced at her, noticing the slight movement. Within minutes, Carol thought about the seven strategies for success discussion that she had heard just a few days earlier. As the governor spoke, Carol gave a powerful and affirmative nod with her head, being ever so slight. The governor immediately looked at her individually. His gaze was for several seconds and Carol said she was taken aback at how powerful she felt. It took her a few minutes to grasp what she was able to do. As the speech went on, the governor looked at her once again, but this time he paused to smile at her. She smiled back and simply looked away. She did this two more times. Each time, the governor looked directly at her. After the speech was finished, Carol rose to her feet and noticed the governor was headed in her direction. About this time she turned to see the governor's hand outstretched. Carol felt embarrassed but was flattered that he had made the gesture. The governor immediately asked if he knew Carol. Carol responded that she had never met him, but commented that she attended a local school and that she was graduating in a few months. The governor said, "I just can't get over why you look so familiar to me." He proceeded to ask about her family and other possible ties. He was sure he knew her from somewhere. Finally, the governor asked Carol if she had a summer job. When she said that she didn't, he grabbed a business card and told her to call his secretary for a summer job. He wrote her name down in his appointment book and said he was looking forward to seeing her working in the statehouse this summer.

When Carol came back to school, she stopped by my room to tell me the story of the governor. She said, "Mr. Brower, you won't believe what happened to me today, but your talk sure works. All I did was nod my head and each time the governor looked directly at me." The good governor probably never understood why he looked at Carol five or more times. All he did was do what comes naturally; that is to look and be attracted to people who listen to us, who agree with us, and who are eager to learn.

The second story involves a boy by the name of Sam. Sam was exposed to the seven strategies for success three different times while a student in Ms. Keller's biology class. Sam left for college and found himself in a very difficult political science class with over 500 students. Sam decided it was time to implement those seven strategies for success with Dr. Mayhern. Sam knew it was time to get to work on this good doctor of political science.

There was no seating chart and as the days went by, fewer and fewer students continued to attend class. Sam came to class every day. Sam never brought negative attention toward himself during class. Sam became a master of the positive head nod. In a 50-minute class, Sam would wait patiently for Dr. Mayhern to look up at the crowd. Every 5 minutes or so, Sam would make eye contact with the professor, each time giving the familiar nod. After 2 weeks, Sam progressed to attending Dr. Mayhern's office hours. Dr. Mayhern immediately complimented Sam on his attending class and listening so intently. Dr. Mayhern invited Sam to lunch and offered Sam the position of teaching assistant.

Needless to say, Sam received an A in class. Dr. Mayhern nominated him for the outstanding senior student academic award. Sam won the award and was later employed by an accounting firm, owned by Dr. Mayhern's father. The joys of positive behavior had helped get Sam a great job and a relationship with Dr. Mayhern.

Numerous stories about the effectiveness of the nod of the head have come back to us via notes and other communication devices. Each time we hear a student share an experience with us, we are more impressed with the power of this simple gesture. We each use it in various facets of life, and the effects have been nothing short of miraculous for us as professionals. Here are a few reports, out of the thousands we have received, from people practicing the technique.

- A girl reported that in church she routinely has the minister look at her, while giving the sermon, simply by nodding her head. He later acknowledged her after the sermon.
- In large lecture halls in college, students report how they can get professors to single them out of the crowd.
- In small groups when someone has to be chosen, the nod of the head will make the person surface quickly out of this group of people.
- Nodding with a police officer after being pulled over has prevented tickets from being written.
- Nodding agreement with parents has lessened discipline.
- Nodding with bosses has led to promotions and better work assignments.
- Students have been selected out of a large crowd to do tasks (during schoolwide assemblies) that require trust.

All of these examples are genuine and illustrate that this simple technique can lead to powerful and positive relationship building. With strong relationship building comes positive success building. These two go hand in hand—the stronger the relationship with a teacher, the greater the possibility of success in the classroom. There is a direct correlation. Motivation can be directly related to the positive experiences students have in classrooms. This increase in motivation will lead to more powerful occurrences!

However, one note of caution should be addressed. A student should only occasionally give a nod of the head. Do not do this continually or in a disrespectful way. When the student nods, he or she should look directly at the teacher or person and give a three-nod positive up and down gesture—no more. This is enough to get the person's attention in a positive way. Continuous nodding and disrespectful nodding can do more harm than good. During any 20-minute segment of listening, a student should not practice this technique more than four or five times. The student should be selective as to when to nod. It is best to nod after hearing something particularly agreeable or interesting.

Obviously, it is important for the student to pay attention to anyone speaking. Listening serves two purposes: first, it will help in understanding the speaker; second, by listening, one avoids the temptation to bring negative attention toward oneself. This is critically important to a student's success in class. The nod of the head takes the listening portion of the relationship one step further. We have said more than once that it is more important to project that we are listening than actually listening. This is not to suggest that it is okay to not listen, but we all understand there are times when listening is not critical to the case at hand. In any case, the student must project all of the time that they are listening. Nodding opens the door to opportunity, while listening gets one inside.

OTHER POSITIVE BODY LANGUAGE

Although the simple affirmative nod of the head sends a very powerful message, there are other body languages and simple behaviors that are just as effective. There are also numerous body languages that should be

Table 5.1.   Effective and Noneffective Body Language Behaviors

Dos	Don'ts
Sit upright in one's seat	Slouch down in one's seat
Make eye contact as often as possible	Keep the head down or stare at the wall/ceiling
Nod the head affirmatively on occasion	Give no positive feedback
Wear acceptable clothing to school	Dress slovenly or with unacceptable/illegal slogans on your clothing
Raise one's hand only after the adult is finished speaking	Raise your hand while the adult is still speaking
Look forward and appear interested	Ignore the speaker or turn your back
Use pleasant facial expressions (like smiling)	Have a disagreeable disposition
Shake hands with adults	Ignore adults when approached
Be on time to class and school	Be tardy or absent (unless absolutely necessary)
Be helpful to others in deeds	Be concerned with oneself only
Volunteer to help the adults in school	Let someone else do the work
Be patient and understanding in actions	Be impatient and lack understanding
Show up and do the work	Be gone when work is needed
Know the difference of when to laugh and when to be serious	Laugh at inappropriate times

avoided. Table 5.1 illustrates both lists. We encourage you to add your own ideas to this list of dos and don'ts.

Many students forget their body language and simple actions can profoundly affect how others perceive them. Once this perception is set in stone, it can be very difficult to overcome and the consequences will often become a self-fulfilling prophecy. This, unfortunately, can spiral the student further into a world devoid of the motivation required to succeed in school and in life.

While researching several books on how children are now motivated, one is struck by the thought that many scholars believe students may not be reaching their potential because educators are not doing things the "right way." This may well be true, but we still believe nearly all students, regardless of their intellectual, cognitive, or behavioral levels can learn and grow in profoundly positive ways if these students learn the basic strategies to be successful. Positive body language can be the start to a very positive personal image. Students can use this positive personal image to further relationships and become successful in various aspects of school and life. For example, numerous books have been written on gifted children, vocationally minded students, special needs students, and how educators are not meeting their needs (Davidson & Davidson, 2004; Yecke, 2005). Indeed, there is no shortage of books advocating this very notion. The point of this chapter is not to dispute those thoughts but rather to take a different approach to how students can reach their full potential by adopting some very simple strategies that will blossom into powerful relationships with teachers that in turn will create a climate of mutual trust and an ensuing explosion of possibilities. Students can help create this climate by participating in positive body language. The teachers will be more likely to produce a fun and exciting classroom environment if the students exhibit a want-to-learn image.

Once teachers and administrators understand how to empower students to learn the strategies behind success in school and life, they can begin to rethink how the key to unlocking learning is not about the subject matter so much as it is about the people. That is the foundation of learning. Once the metaphoric foundation is constructed by teaching students the seven strategies, then the house of eventual success will surely follow. Teaching students the power of positive body language is but one tool in this process.

6

STRATEGY 5: THE POWER OF SMALL, POSITIVE BEHAVIORS AND ACTIONS

Those who bring sunshine to the lives of others cannot keep it from themselves.

—James Barrie

Strategy 5 outlines another great way for students to build strong relationships with teachers and peers. This strategy is often difficult for students to accept outwardly because it may appear to them that this positive practice is "brown nosing." Nothing could be further from the truth. The practice can become second nature once learned and developed and will lead to positive character development by illustrating giving and service to others. Strategy 5 follows the previous strategies and will further construct the dispositions necessary to achieve success in school.

Most students have not yet learned the basic principles of behavior that are widely accepted as good character traits that will empower students to become successful. These behaviors are simple in nature and easy to implement. The question remains, however, if these behaviors are so easy to implement, why isn't everyone motivated to begin implementing this good trait? The answer is both complex and simple.

The complexity comes when trying to understand human behavior and how people react to various people and situations. The simple part of the explanation is that most people are not taught the strategies to become better people. As simple as the ideas are, their implementation can be more difficult. These success strategies are rarely taught to students in any formal setting.

Occasionally, religions will teach values and character traits, but even these can fall far short of helping students to understand the profound positive benefits of acting in appropriate ways. The behaviors and actions offered in this chapter are very simple yet powerful methodologies that work. Once perfected, these strategies act as motivators to the students as well as to teachers, administrators, and other adults in the school setting. Nearly all people enjoy being the recipient of positive acts of appreciation. These actions will create an exponential explosion of goodwill within the entire school family!

Most people understand the power of positive actions, words, and behaviors but few actually practice the behaviors or actions long enough to make them habits. Although the number of positive actions or behaviors a person can perform is infinitesimal, we offer a few that are extremely effective in the school setting. Once a person learns these basic positive behaviors, it will be amazing to see the acceleration of how these are used with even newer and more creative ideas that will complement the character development of the student.

POSITIVE BEHAVIOR I

Always give a salutation to your teacher every single day, every period of the day. This extends to the principals, custodians, cafeteria workers, aides, and support staff. Greet these people enthusiastically every single day with a "Hi," "Howdy," or "How are you doing today?" The salutation can be said in any number of ways, but the effect is the same. It must be done respectfully and appear genuine and sincere. It is important that the adult feels venerated in the exchange and not belittled in any way (as if being made a subject of ridicule). It is interesting how a positive gesture coming from a student who has a history of querulous misbehavior can be misinterpreted so easily. It is very important that the student comes across as credible to the teacher or administrator.

The second part of this behavior is saying goodbye every single day, every single period of the day to the teachers as well as any other adult in the school. Saying hi and goodbye is powerful in building relationships. It pronounces that you like the person you are addressing; you enjoy being in his or her company; and that you are a friendly and positive person. All of these actions make for building great relationships and will lead to positive results.

We are appalled at the number of students who come to school every day and never once say hi or goodbye to any adult in the school. It is easy to see why students often feel the adults are the "enemy." We all know this is nonsense, but this feeling permeates the minds of many students. Also, many students' perception of doing things for teachers is unacceptable to their peers. It is considered brown nosing or being a teacher's "pet." Truth is, teachers will rarely, if ever, think a student is trying to "suck-up," they will usually believe the student is a nice young man or woman.

When the student forces him- or herself to be friendly and ebullient to the teachers and administrators in the building (in fact, any adult in the building) it helps create a positive working (and learning) environment. In no time, the students and adults in the building will be displaying an air of friendliness never witnessed before. This technique will pay huge dividends for the student. He or she may never tangibly understand it, but the results will be the same. The teacher will try to make the student happy whenever humanly possible. In general, teachers long to please their students, but they appreciate those who show them caring even more. Practicing this behavior works wonders. Before long, other students begin displaying this urbanity of behavior. Here is an example of this principle.

Matt was an average student in a middle school art class. He came into the classroom every day much like each previous day—his head down as he walked past the teacher, rarely saying a word. After he heard the first talk given by Dr. Brower on the strategies listed in this book, he started saying hi and goodbye to every adult in the building. After several days of this behavior, he stopped by Dr. Brower's room to discuss the transformation in his relationship with adults in the building. Matt talked about how everyone was suddenly so friendly toward him and that he no longer viewed the principal as a "scary guy."

One day the principal actually invited him to his office just to talk. From that day forward, Matt made a point to say hi to the principal every single day. Matt shared this story and many more of its kind. Matt continued to practice this strategy and realized the potential of his success. Matt went on to Harvard University and is now a medical doctor. He routinely contacts Dr. Brower and mentions how much of his success he directly attributes to his change of personality brought on by implementing the seven strategies for success in school and in life.

POSITIVE BEHAVIOR 2

Always limit comments to positive ones. Simply put: if you do not have anything nice to say, don't say anything at all. Here is a small sample of common phrases that we have heard students using:

- I love this class.
- You are my favorite teacher.
- I love math . . .
- This is my best/favorite period of the day.
- You make learning fun and exciting.
- What would I do without this class?
- I will miss you next term/year.
- Would it be possible for you to get me in your class next term/year?
- Thanks/thank you/I appreciate it.
- What can I do to help you?

These phrases are but a few of the hundreds that can be used daily as motivation for every student and the teachers. These will give the teacher the sense that the student is a positive person who really enjoys the class and them, as a person. Once again, this builds positive relationships, and positive teacher relationships lead to success.

POSITIVE BEHAVIOR 3

Give small tokens of appreciation to others. This is another behavior often ignored by students. Many students will refuse to use this effective behavior for fear that teachers will misinterpret the intention as being one of self-ingratiation. Once again, nothing could be further from the truth. Teachers love this behavior because students so rarely practice it at any level. Teachers are motivated to improve teaching methods, which in turn, motivates all students to learn.

The behavior can be utilized by simply leaving a note, a card, a small present, some candy, or some token of appreciation for what the teacher has done. For example, a student is having a tough time with math. A note to the teacher saying something like, "You are the best math teacher I have ever had, but I still have trouble understanding story problems. I do my homework every night, but I still have trouble understanding how to put words into math. Would it be possible for me to stay after school to get some help or could you give me some recommendation on how better to understand these problems?" These notes can include simple sayings such as:

- Thank you for all that you do to make this class fun and enjoyable.
- You are my favorite teacher this year.
- Have a great weekend Miss Martin.
- Enjoy the holiday break—you deserve it for all your hard work.
- Sorry I messed up on the last test, I'll study harder next time—it was my fault.
- Smile!
- Class was great today. Can't wait until tomorrow.

These notes convey an unbelievable level of powerful, motivational, and positive reinforcement. The teacher will cherish these small tokens of affection for life. Oftentimes educators will keep these tokens to remind them of the "good times." Teachers need and require positive reinforcement, just as students long for it. Therefore, by giving these tokens, students and teachers both benefit from the interaction.

Homemade Christmas cards, Hanukkah cards, Valentine's cards, Halloween cards, candy, treats, and small gifts all help put the student ahead of the crowd. When practicing these behaviors, the student will quickly discover the profound positive effect it will have on relationship building. Once again, strong relationships with people who teach and have control over your success will breed positive long-term success.

It is very important that teachers and administrators help students understand that this practice is *not* about "buying" affection, grades, or
brown nosing, but rather about learning the art of giving rather than re-
ceiving. This practice helps nurture positive character traits and teaches
students the profound enlightenment and satisfaction of giving and serving others. Sergiovanni (1992, 1994, 2000) talks about these dispositions
in teachers and administrators. These same behavioral traits work just as
effectively with students.

POSITIVE BEHAVIOR 4

Everyone should practice random acts of kindness whenever possible.
These acts should be practiced not only toward teachers, but also toward
as many acquaintances as humanly possible. Students could volunteer to
help the teacher pass school papers back to students; help the teacher
put up signs or bulletin boards; volunteer to take something to the office for the teacher; help the teacher decorate the room; help the
teacher take down items from the wall; erase the board; or move the
desks and chairs when appropriately asked. If someone drops something, a student should help pick it up before being asked to do so. If
someone is down, the student should be taught to be kind, polite, and
lend a helping hand. If the student sees a teacher or person in need of
help, he or she should not wait to be asked to help. Instead, the student
should be ready to volunteer immediately when the need arises.

In terms of our own family, several examples come to mind. My son
Adam was having trouble with a middle school teacher when he was in
sixth grade. This teacher was loathed by seemingly all of her students.
Early in the second term, Adam came home daily with stories of this
teacher's shortcomings. He indicated that he didn't care if she liked him
or not, he just wanted to get out of her class.

Although my son had never actually heard the seven strategies to success talk in my classroom, he had heard me preach the positive behaviors espoused in this book. I convinced him to practice positive words
and behaviors, along with the other strategies I share with students.
These strategies were working, but the turning point came during the
holiday season. Adam was still struggling with the concept of trying to

build a relationship with someone he did not respect. I kept telling him that these are the people we need to work the hardest on to achieve success. Participating in these behaviors and actions are necessary to achieve success.

I bought his teacher a Cross-pen set; my wife and I made Adam wrap the present, despite his protests. Not knowing what was in the package, Mrs. Truman said thank you to Adam as he scurried out the door. We would later learn that this was the only present this teacher had received in her 22 years as an educator. Adam delivered his other presents and returned to Mrs. Truman's class where she was waiting for him. She ran at him with her arms stretched out and grabbed him around the waist, picked him up off the ground, and twirled him around in circles. From that day forward, Adam had a lifelong friend.

Students should be made aware that these types of "gifts" are not akin to trying to purchase grades. The intent in practicing these behaviors and actions is to promote giving and encourage service to others. When these behaviors are learned and implemented in students' daily lives, they become motivated to do even more for people once the rewards of these behaviors are reciprocated to them.

Gifts such as fancy pens are not necessary; it is not the cost of the item but rather the intent of giving and kindness. Simple actions that cost little money and time are excellent ways to learn the positive character trait of giving to others. These practices will invariably give an array of joy to others. The message with this strategy must be very clear—build a beautiful habit of success by being kind, giving to others, being generous to all, and caring toward one's fellow man (woman). Small tokens of appreciation can go a long way to help build these positive, caring relationships with adults and to nurture positive character traits.

In our years as teachers, coaches, and administrators, we have received thousands of notes, tokens of appreciation, and cards. We possess large boxes and scrapbooks filled with these notes, cards, and keepsakes from over 15,000 students. On those dismal days, when all seems dreary and negative, those boxes of cards and notes are opened and reread. These gestures, although simple in content, are full of emotion and remembrance of a time when teaching was a career, not just a job. Everyone should have a box of positives to revisit from time to time. It is good for the soul.

❼

STRATEGY 6:
THE POWER OF PRACTICING
"MIRROR RELATIONSHIP BUILDING"

You must be the change you wish to see in the world.

—Gandhi

Mirror relationship building simply means mimicking (mirroring) those behaviors you see in yourself and others that you would like to see everyone emulate. If a person is seen performing an act of kindness, the witness to this act can reciprocate the behavior (like a mirror) and demonstrate the same behavior to someone else. By modeling positive traits in others, one can incrementally adopt those behaviors as one's own. Most experts agree that to break a habit or to form new habits takes at least 6 to 8 weeks of diligent effort (Braden, 1993). As easily as bad habits are formed, new habits and behaviors can just as easily be adopted as a part of our personality and character.

The Golden Rule

Do unto others just as you
Would like for them to do unto you
Listen with care, but do not dare
To tell someone else what to do

Be gentle and kind, and soon you will find
That they will be the same way with you.

—Annette L. Breaux,
The Poetry of Annette Breaux

Some people call this behavior the Golden Rule: Do unto others as you would have them do unto you. The Golden Rule is a religious message, in some form, passed down through the ages in nearly every acceptable world religion. Regardless of one's religion or belief system, practicing what we call "mirror relationship building" is essential to sustained happiness and success. Treat others in ways you find appealing and effective, without wanting something in return. By mirroring these positive behaviors, a person will quickly discover he or she is happier and more successful. Before long, these new practiced behaviors will become a part of the brain's "hard drive" and, thus, hardwired into a person's thought processes. These new and improved habits will involuntarily be portrayed in your daily actions.

In addition to the aforementioned thought, another phenomenon worth mentioning is the idea that one negative behavior can wipe out hundreds of good deeds or words. For example, one angry word spoken in haste can destroy a friendship that has developed over years.

A story we often tell to explain this point is an analogy of human nature. I jog regularly, and everyday when I leave my house I take the same route out of my neighborhood. This route takes me on the same path along the street, over a small bridge, and onto a sidewalk on the other side of the creek that separates two housing developments. I had taken the same path hundreds of times, when on one occasion, I was startled by a snake near the sidewalk. Just as I approached the far edge of the sidewalk, the startled snake, in a defensive reaction, reared its head and lunged toward me. I nearly jumped out of my skin. Seeing a snake in that location was completely unexpected.

Even though I had traveled that same path hundreds of times before, I had never once seen a snake or expected to see one. Interestingly, now, every time I go by that same spot, I look for that snake. Many times I will avoid the spot of the encounter by jogging on the other side of the road. One thing is certain, however: I look for that snake every time I pass that sidewalk.

This story illustrates how one awful experience can overpower hundreds of positive experiences. This fundamental law of human nature reaffirms the need to constantly treat people with the dignity and respect they deserve, lest we destroy a relationship because of one indiscretion. The way in which a teacher/administration handles a potential indiscretion with a student or colleague is critically important to salvaging the future relationship with that person. All educators should remember this simple truth.

The following story concerns a student who was unfortunately enrolled in a classroom where the teacher did not understand the importance of relationship building. A freshman biology teacher told me this very disheartening story during my sixth year of teaching. After hearing it I was incredibly motivated to improve my relationship with students through the communication of this story.

John was 7 years old when his father acquired his pilot's license. To celebrate this acquisition, John and his father flew (over a 3-day weekend) to Las Vegas. After the weekend, the students returned to school and talked about what they had done over the weekend. It soon became John's turn to brag about his weekend. John began a story most students would be enamored to learn. John told of a weekend of fun, excitement, and overnight flights to Las Vegas and home again.

After class, John's teacher called him to her desk and had a detention written. On the detention, the teacher had written, "John lied during class today." John asked the teacher what she was talking about; he had no recollection of lying. She had informed him that his story about flying to Las Vegas was surely a lie; after all, no one could fly to Las Vegas and back in a matter of three days. John continued to proclaim his innocence, while the teacher escorted him to the principal's office.

After two conferences with the principal, John's parents were called. John's father assured the principal that yes, indeed, they had flown to Las Vegas and that John was not lying. Unfortunately, the damage was already done. John had begun to speak less during class; after this fiasco, John waited until my class to speak again. Fortunately, I encouraged John and his parents to, once again, develop positive relationships with teachers.

Numerous stories come to mind to illustrate this mirror relationship building phenomenon that we all need to practice to be happier and more successful. By practicing this behavior daily, the change will soon become embedded in our actions and will shine through in others' reciprocal reactions to our positive behaviors.

Another story is told to show the importance of relationship building. Imagine a sixth-grade boy who ran to biology class everyday because one of his former teachers had put an unforgiving fear in him. On the first day of the third grading period, I watched him sprint from my room and down the hallway headed to his next class. In a matter of seconds, I witnessed several freshmen students knock all of his books from his arms and onto the floor. Several teachers rushed to his aid.

The freshmen culprits were laughing and kicking the boy's books down the ramp just as the teachers arrived on the scene. The boys scattered at the sight of us arriving, all the while we tried to console the young boy. Tears were frantically falling from his face as I helped him gather his papers and books. Almost immediately, I noticed two cheerleaders bent over helping the boy pick up his scattered belongings. The girls were consoling him by patting him on the back, telling him to ignore the boys and forget their raucous behavior.

Fortunately enough, one of the girls offered to walk him to his next class. I offered to accompany the girl and this student to class. The young boy stopped by my classroom later the next day to thank me for my kindness. I had made a friendly relationship that would endure throughout the boy's entire junior high career. The mirror relationship building was alive and well.

We recall another incident that involved a freshman football player and a seventh-grade student at her school that illustrates how it is always best to treat people well regardless of our position. The freshman quarterback was walking with two other football players down the junior high corridors when a seemingly wimpy seventh grader was heading right toward their triumphant position. The seventh-grade boy was not paying attention because he was half turned talking to a girl going the other direction. Just as the younger boy reached the three football players, the quarterback knocked the shoulder and side of the head of the seventh grader.

The attack was vicious enough to knock the young boy to the ground. The three freshman boys continued walking and laughing. The young boy immediately rose and chased after his attackers. As the seventh-grade boy confronted the freshman, he proceeded to poke his finger in the chest of the quarterback and said, "Do you wanna fight?" The quarterback shot back a time and place of the supposed fight. As the day wore on, the quarterback began hearing stories about how this kid was a good fighter. Suddenly, the odds didn't appear quite so overwhelming, but the quarterback's confidence was still intact, although somewhat shaky now.

After school, the word about a fight after school had spread and there were at least a hundred students assembled in the city park adjoining the school. Just as everyone was giving up hope that the younger boy would show, the boy (with six other seventh graders huddled closely behind) began walking toward the large crowd. The boy had no sooner gotten to the park boundaries when he began dancing around and holding his fists outward. Suddenly, the young boy punched the right eye of the quarterback, sending him reeling backward. Again, he hit the older boy while another hit landed squarely on the older boy's nose. The quarterback lay on the ground stunned and in agony. Blood covered the football player's face.

The stunned football team could do little more than look on in awe. The quarterback walked home by himself in total humiliation. He missed several days of school until he was forced to return and face the humiliation of what he had created. To add insult to injury, he eventually lost his starting position to another player. The coach was disgusted with his continued bad attitude.

This story illustrates how important it is to treat everyone with the dignity each person deserves. It also illustrates the truly unmotivating effect that negative and degrading behavior can have on an adult or child. We should treat the weak like the strong and forgive those who are often vexatious to us. Mirror the behaviors in others that you yourself enjoy, admire, and are motivated by; forget those behaviors that you are angered by, unmotivated by, or saddened by.

This is a story of Bob, a jealous senior, and Ron, an innocent, friendly classmate. Bob was the jealous type who demanded that other guys stay away from his beautiful girlfriend. Judy, his girlfriend, was troubled by Bob's obsessive behavior, but tolerated it because she loved him. Ron was in two of Judy's classes. Judy had no romantic interest in Ron, but Ron was one of those young men who was friendly with everyone.

On numerous occasions, Ron would walk with Judy to their next class. One day though, Bob happened to come to school late and was waiting at the stairs for Judy when he saw Ron and Judy walking together and laughing. Bob became enraged and quickly made it clear to Ron to stay away from Judy. Judy was extremely embarrassed and told Bob that his actions were nothing short of total silliness. Bob promised to work on his temper and for the time being, the incident was over.

Three days later, Bob happened to catch Judy and Ron together once again walking to class and their shoulders were touching in the crowded hallway. Bob snapped and immediately ran at Ron. Bob shouted out that if he saw Ron outside of school, he would surely fight him. Ron hurriedly murmured that he was sorry if had done anything wrong and that he meant nothing by his innocent actions with Judy. Bob then turned and yanked Judy by the arm and began pulling her down the hallway.

A few days later after school, Ron was walking out the doors of school and Judy just happened to be a few students behind him. Bob, in the outside courtyard, just happened to glance in the direction of Judy when he spotted Ron close behind. In Bob's insecure mind, he assumed they were conspiring to be together.

Bob worked his way through the mass of students and headed directly toward Ron. Ron had gone down the steps and was making his way to the candy shop across the street. Just as Ron walked through the door and to the counter, he heard someone say his name. Hearing his name, Ron turned to look back toward the door for confirmation. Just as Ron was turning around, Bob hit Ron squarely between the eyes.

The blow was so vicious that it knocked Ron backward into the candy case, shattering the glass panels. Bob stepped back and seemed shocked at what he had just done. The young lady behind the counter screamed at Bob to stop as she stepped in front of the candy case to protect Ron from further harm. The saleslady immediately dialed the police dispatcher while Ron made his way to his feet. Within minutes, two police vehicles arrived and Bob was put in handcuffs. Ron was taken to the hospital. Thankfully, Ron was not seriously hurt.

As a disciplinary action, Bob was required to pay for the repair of the candy case. In addition, Bob was suspended from school for five days and was required to give Ron a handwritten apology. Bob regretted his actions and apologized to Judy, but the damage had already been done. Judy refused to talk to Bob ever again and their relationship ended that day.

Twenty-five years later at a class reunion, Bob made his peace with Ron. It was the first time the two had ever really discussed the unfortunate incident back in high school. Ron and Bob had missed each other at previous reunions. Bob offered his profound and sincere apologies to Ron in an effort to put finality on the incident. The past had successfully and finally been put to rest.

This story again illustrates how people can act in counterproductive and damaging ways. No one gains an advantage or wins a fight by committing hurtful actions or deeds toward others. Practicing mirror relationship building creates strong and healthy bonds between people and nurtures strong interpersonal relationships.

As Steven Covey (1990) writes in his book *Principle-Centered Leadership*, people should strive to place "deposits" in people's emotional "bank accounts" and, therefore, when a "withdrawal" is needed, there should be enough deposits to cover the needed "withdrawal." The practice of abiding by the Golden Rule is a simple concept, but many people have trouble understanding the power behind this universally accepted concept. By mirroring others exemplary behaviors and actions, a person can grow in incredibly positive ways. Mirroring others can be a truly rewarding experience for everyone. The Golden Rule has been witnessed throughout the history of the world and is a uniquely human trait.

Encourage your students to emulate the behaviors of others they deem appropriate, positive, and admirable. Once the desired behaviors are identified, the student, teacher, or administrator can then begin the 6- to 8-week period necessary to proactively change his or her brain's "hard drive" of actions to more rewarding and successful habits (Braden, 1993).

Mirror relationship building is yet another critical puzzle piece that can lead to a productive and successful lifestyle. Unfortunately, more recently this mirroring process (negative influence) behavior has shifted from a focus on positive behavior to a focus on negative (more costly) behaviors. Teens are attempting to model drug/alcohol use, deadly stunts seen on television, and lucrative sex acts. This is why the professional relationship with students is vital to their success and the students' choice to mirror positive, admirable traits. This is a critical distinction for young adults to remember! While mirroring personality and character traits can be both motivating and rewarding, students need to realize the importance of choosing positive, exemplary, and constructive behaviors to model and not choose destructive models to emulate. It is critical that educational professionals make this important distinction with all students.

⑧

STRATEGY 7:
THE POWER OF UNDERSTANDING
AND ACCEPTING CONSEQUENCES
OF YOUR ACTIONS

Events, circumstances, and consequences have their origin in ourselves. They spring from seeds, which we have sown.

—Henry David Thoreau

This is the final strategy on the road to success. The length of this chapter is directly proportional to its importance. The strategy in this chapter is much more involved than the previous strategies and thus much more emphasis is placed on this strategy. In some ways, this strategy protects students from themselves and their often destructive behaviors. Students' destructive behaviors fall into two distinctly different arenas: the type a person has control over and the type a person cannot control. This chapter will make those distinctions and will then offer a proven strategy to keep students from harm's way.

Before we extol the virtues of Strategy 7, it is important for young people to understand the two distinct ways tragedies can occur. One is usually out of our control; the second we can certainly control through our thought and decision-making processes. Students should use these strategies to motivate their future decisions and endeavors.

ACCIDENTAL TRAGEDIES: OUTSIDE OF OUR CONTROL

The first kind of tragedy is accidental in nature; the person being hurt is simply in the wrong place at the wrong time. Even if one party could have prevented the accident or event, many times the other party is simply there when the tragedy manifests itself. Every day hundreds of people are killed, injured, or are a part of a tragedy. These may occur because a person was at a certain intersection or place when another person decides to run a light, which almost always ends in tragedy. The innocent person did not know what was about to happen and thus could not avoid it.

How many times have we avoided tragedy because we stopped to use the bathroom before we left the house, got caught by a stop light, waited for a person to cross the road before we proceeded, got in the wrong line at the store, or slowed down to change the radio on our car? No one can tell if the avoidance of tragedy happened because we were not in a certain place at a certain time. If a person knew the tragedy was about to happen, that person would surely take the corrective measures to avoid the tragedy.

The types of incidents beyond our control are called ignorance. Ignorance is not a bad word; it simply implies not knowing something. Chapter 2 of this book discusses ignorance and stupidity more in depth. When we get up in the morning, any potential tragedy can lie ahead without a shred of forethought or foreseeability. The following are two examples we give to illustrate how this type of tragedy can occur without warning.

The first is an example of an innocent person being involved in a serious tragedy without any prior knowledge. Randy's dad had just bought him a new 1967 Mustang. His dad bartered with Randy to give up his Triumph motorcycle because the father felt the motorcycle was an accident waiting to happen. Randy and his girlfriend met for dinner and a movie. After the late movie, Randy and Sarah talked for about an hour in her driveway just past the edge of town. They were getting to know one another and shared some funny stories.

At just past midnight, Sarah's dad blinked the porch light to signal it was time for Sarah to come inside. Randy walked around to open the car door for Sarah and they walked to the porch to say goodbye. Randy turned and made his way to the car, as Sarah waited in the doorway. As Randy pulled out onto the country road, he hesitated, leaned over to roll the window down, and waved with his right hand out the window as the car began to move forward. All of a sudden Sarah saw lights coming over the hill just behind Randy's car.

This area of the road was hidden in a valley with the hill just high enough to block the view of oncoming cars. The man in the GTO was going over 70 miles per hour and could not stop in time. Randy's Mustang was hit—blind-sided by the GTO. Sarah watched in horror as she stood helpless in the doorway. The collision was so devastating that Randy's car was thrown into the air and landed 30 feet down the road. Sarah came out of the house screaming. Her dad was up, heard the crash, and immediately called for an ambulance.

Sarah was totally distraught as she frantically searched for Randy in the darkness. Sarah's mother tried to console her as the ambulance could be heard echoing in the distance. Sarah's dad looked for Randy but he was not in his vehicle or anywhere in sight. Sarah and her dad wondered what had happened to him. By now the entire row of houses had people coming outside to see what had happened.

Randy's body was finally found around 6:00 A.M. about 70 feet away in the cornfield across the road from Sarah's house. Randy was so badly injured that his body could not be viewed at the funeral home. His dad identified him at the morgue. Could this accident have been prevented? There is no question that Randy's lack of stopping at the road contributed to the accident. However, think of all the scenarios that had to coincidentally occur to make these two vehicles hit at just that fateful moment in time. Was it fate? Was it destiny? No one can really assess those questions, but the fact remains that no one could predict or prepare for this kind of accidental tragedy.

This story illustrates the frustration of these kinds of tragedies; maybe they could have been prevented. Nonetheless, the fact remains clear that these tragedies will happen every day in our culture. They are unfortunate and sad, despite the lesson being learned.

A second story involves a beautiful young lady named Mary. Mary was driving home from her softball game in her new car. As she crested the hill, she noticed the light was about to turn green so she didn't slow down. Surely she could time the light change. She timed it perfectly and entered the intersection just as the light turned green. Just then, she caught the lights of a tanker semi coming directly at her. She turned just briefly before the impact.

Mary was killed instantly. It took 3 hours to free Mary from the wreckage. Her parents, who had been called by a teammate following Mary, had come to the site of the accident. The truck driver and witnesses said there was nothing that could have prevented the accident; the truck was loaded with supplies and could not stop when the light changed to yellow. Mary could not see the intersection because of trees blocking the coming traffic. The driver of the truck was only going 50 miles per hour.

This is yet another anecdote that illustrates how vulnerable everyone is to tragic accidents beyond our control. Heart attacks, industrial accidents, natural disasters, and any number of other maladies can cause tragedies. With vigilance and proactive measures, many tragedies can be avoided. The sad fact is our world will never be completely safe and that certain innocent people will always be dealt tragedies beyond their control. These types of everyday tragedies cannot accurately be predicted or adequately prevented. These types of tragedies are a part of our existence and we cannot allow ourselves to worry about one of these unfortunate incidents confronting us. We simply have to live our lives in ways that keep these tragedies to a minimum. Unfortunately, one may still fall victim to this phenomenon.

STUDENT-CONTROLLED TRAGEDIES

In addition to the tragedies out of our control, students may fall victim to the second type of tragedy, those that students can control. These tragedies are often more tragic in nature because everyone involved in the mourning process realizes the choices the young adults had made. A young adult's choices can be detrimental to his or her life or future. These tragedies can clearly be prevented and thus warrant deep consideration of understanding.

The second kind of tragedy involves stupidity. Stupidity is a derogatory word, which means we have prior knowledge of the situation and choose to ignore it to our own potential detriment. Students may knowingly choose this route because of the potential thrill, high, or peer acceptance associated with the decision. This chapter is devoted to avoiding these types of behaviors and actions that can lead to the second type of tragedy. Stupidity means we can choose another behavior or action that will avoid tragedy or harm. Our thoughts dictate our feelings, our feelings dictate our actions, and our actions dictate our behaviors, which in turn develop our habits of living.

For example, it is impossible to see if someone is angry without seeing his or her actions. Only then can we make a determination that they are angry. This is true of all emotions. Emotions are powerful and lead to actions and behaviors that can be positive or destructive in nature. We call this out-of-control or destructive behavior an expansion of our horizons or boundaries in negative ways. Our challenge as human beings is to allow ourselves to grow in positive ways and to control our expansion in negative ways.

An example of how one grows in positive ways is to examine how an infant develops incrementally the ability to roll over, then to crawl, then to stand, then to walk, then to run, then to sprint, then to leave the house on his or her own, to visit neighbors and friends without supervision, to riding his or her bike across town, to driving hundreds of miles without help, to moving out on his or her own only to start the process again with his or her own kids. This is true in nearly every aspect of our lives from personal to professional endeavors. These should be encouraged in every sense of the word. Learning new courses, speaking new languages, learning new skills, lifelong learning initiatives, and self-help programs all are examples of how we grow as people.

But just as easily as it is to grow in these positive ways, a person can grow in negative ways as well. These negative growth patterns often lead to destructive and tragic consequences. We can control these growth patterns as parents with our kids, as teachers with our students, or simply as people controlling ourselves. But to understand how this negative growth takes place, we must understand what leads to this negative growth.

Here is a list of some ways that facilitate negative growth or dispositions on the part of individuals:

- A lack of supervision by older and more trusted adults.
- The negative influence of another person. This can be a peer, friend, family member, or adult.

- No clear-cut expectations or boundaries set forth.
- Little/no discipline in our own lives, or little/no discipline placed on our loved ones or those under our influence.
- A lack of humanity toward others.
- A lack of a conscience.
- A lack of remorse or feelings toward other people or animals.
- Unrepentant behaviors.
- Unchecked hatred.
- A lack of values and morals.
- Peer pressure.
- Rebellion against authority.

The next story will illustrate how any person is potentially vulnerable to traveling down roads that lead to tragedy. If people are not able to control themselves, their horizons can be expanded in negative ways that harm themselves and others.

Two young inner-city boys, Henri, 11, and Micah, 9, were living in the government-provided projects of a large eastern city. It was a hot summer day when the two boys spotted a 6-year-old boy and his 8-year-old brother throwing rocks at a trash container. When the older boys wandered upon the younger boys, they confronted them about their destructive behavior. The youngest boy turned, threw a rock at the two older boys, and started to run. He was caught hiding under an old abandoned car hood leaning next to a tree.

The boys yanked him out from under the car hood. Henri and Micah covered his mouth and told him if he continued to scream, they would beat him up. Henri grabbed the young boy's belt from behind and took him to the roof of a nine-story apartment building. Fortunately for them, no one witnessed the activity.

Henri and Micah then discussed how to handle the insubordinate young boy. They told the young boy to crawl over the edge of the building, to ascend the fire escape below. The little boy would have nothing of it. He started to run. He was quickly caught and returned to the edge. His kicking and thrashing was no match for the older boys. His older brother was below on the ground and started to yell. Immediately both Micah and Henri heaved the little boy over the edge.

The little boy fell, hitting his head, killing him instantly. The older boys ran down the stairs and headed to an arcade about a mile away. After all, to them the young boy was a mere stranger, a meaningless entity, a helpless person who had dared to annoy them, and a throwaway person who dared to defy their orders. Fortunately, both boys were apprehended within minutes.

Upon further investigation, it was discovered that these boys did not "suddenly" become criminal killers. Their past behaviors led to this tragic evolution of criminal and destructive behavior. Both boys had dropped a small, butterscotch-colored hamster from the same roof two weeks earlier. Then, they found a neighborhood cat and tossed it from the roof as well. The two boys then progressed to throwing a puppy from the roof. All animals eventually died from their injuries. The boys buried each animal and not a single adult was aware of their unbelievably horrible behavior. If someone had been supervising the boys or had witnessed the first instance, maybe the boys could have been made to understand the consequences of such malicious behavior.

Both Micah and Henri told the authorities they really didn't think the drop from the building would kill the young boy. They said they did it because he mouthed off to them and was throwing rocks. These boys pushed their boundaries in negative ways and the results were devastating for both them and the boy. If only someone had controlled these boys' insidious descent into criminal activity, maybe they would have grown into productive adults.

Hundreds of similar stories can be told of how individuals or groups of people march down roads that lead to increasingly more destruction. People must control themselves or others will take on the discipline required to control their behavior. Proper civility and societal etiquette can either be a choice by an individual or will become a forced consequence inflicted by another. Anyone is capable of destructive or sinful behavior; each person must be vigilant to the traps of expanding one's horizons in negative ways.

The final story is a perfect example of how any child can begin to progress in ways that expand his or her horizon in a negative fashion if the child is not vigilant to what can and does happen in everyday life. This story describes how behavior can be detrimental to not only the individual, but to others as well.

I was 9 years old when I was finally able to convince my parents to buy me a BB gun for Christmas. On Christmas morning my dad sat me down with a stern lecture that I was only to shoot at the paper targets that came with the gun. Dad had placed two bales of straw outside the back of the garage.

After the presents were opened, Dad and I ventured outside to practice and to learn the strategies of BB gun protocol. Dad instructed me to never point at a person or animal; never to point it toward a house; never to threaten anyone with it; and never to look into the barrel. He cautioned me to watch for the ricochet and showed me what he meant by firing at a piece of plywood. Dad fired, and surely enough, the BB ricocheted off the wood and planted solidly in the side of Blacky's (our beagle's) doghouse. I was impressed with my dad's knowledge and the power of my new weapon.

Dad soon left me to shoot alone and it didn't take long for me to become bored with paper targets. Within a week, I was shooting at passing airplanes, lining up pop bottles on the fence post, shooting holes in tin cans, and routinely carrying my gun into the nearby woods to look for innocent, wild victims. My BB gun was my constant companion, and I was fortunate enough to escape injury. My parents knew I was progressing but rarely spoke about my use of the gun.

One Saturday morning in the spring, I was marching around the side of the house when I noticed a mother bird in her nest feeding her young chicks. The nest was neatly resting on the telephone wire above our house. I maneuvered around until I could get a clear shot at the mother bird. I fired; the shot hit her in the neck, and she dropped from the nest to the ground below. She was dead! When I was confident she was lifeless, I turned my attention to the babies above.

Suddenly it struck me; I had just killed the mother and the babies would not have a mother. I threw my gun down in disgust as I began to cry uncontrollably at my childish and hedonistic behavior. I ran into the house and spotted my mother at the sink. I ran full tilt into her back and grabbed her around the waist and sobbed that I had done something terrible. Mom finally consoled me enough to take me out back.

After a stern lecture on killing for joy, she consoled me as a loving mother does, all the while emphasizing a most important teaching moment. She retrieved an old cigar box from the garage and gently placed tissue on the inside. My two sisters and I placed the box into our Radio Flyer wagon and headed toward the woods to bury the mother bird. My lesson was learned but more needless agony lay ahead.

Later, after school was out for summer, I was in my room. I had just cleaned out my gun and had it standing in the corner next to my bed. I was enjoying a Superman comic when my sister's friend Becky came into my room. After Becky entered the room, my sister bolted in and started messing with my comic books. She said I had taken her brush from her room and she was looking for it. I picked up my BB gun and told them both to leave or I would shoot them. As I pointed toward my sister's midsection and aimed, Becky said, "You're too stupid to pull the trigger." I turned the gun toward Becky's head and said, "Get out now!" When they refused to leave, I pulled the trigger, thinking the noise would scare them off.

Just as I pulled the trigger, a BB flew out and hit Becky in the face. She grabbed her eye with both hands and yelled. Clella, my sister, turned and looked hysterically at Becky's head. Blood was trickling from between her fingers and was running down Becky's face and throat. Clella screamed. Dad bolted upstairs to see what had happened. As soon as my dad saw Becky, he called for Mom to get up stairs quickly.

Mom was already outside the room when Dad lunged at me with madness welling in his eyes. I had never seen this look before on my dad's face. Dad grabbed the gun from my bed, bent it in half, and threw it out the window. He then yanked me off the bed by the upper arm and, just as suddenly, knocked me back onto the bed as he headed out the door with the admonition that I not leave. All I saw out the window through drenched, crying eyes, was our family station wagon kicking up dirt flying down the alley apparently heading to the hospital. I was left at home by myself to await the agonizing truth and the carnage that surely would follow.

Several hours passed as my anxiety level continued to rise. I decided to go outside and wait for my parents' return. I was too stressed to eat, too nervous to watch television, and too scared to talk on the phone. I thought that the neighbors would keep my dad from beating me if I were in the backyard where they could see me if my dad decided to thrash me. Finally, I saw the family car pull into the alley leading to our driveway. My dad spotted me in the yard. As the car slowed to a stop, my stomach turned sour with fright. My mom and sister were first out of the car. Neither my mother nor my sister bothered to look in my direction. I was hoping desperately for some simple sign that I could grasp as impending disaster loomed heavily.

My attention quickly turned to my dad as he slammed the car door shut and headed directly toward me. His pace was one of pure intent. I started crying and began backing up not knowing exactly what would happen. I knew better than to run; I had to take my medicine. Dad grabbed me by the arm, twirled me around, and began flogging me with his belt. I took off running toward the patio door leading to the house. As I opened the door, I fell to the floor. I still did not know the fate of Becky. The answer was not to be known by me for hours. Outside on the grass lay my crumpled BB gun, uselessly begging to be discarded without fanfare or remorse lest it hurt someone else.

As the hours passed, my head began to pound as I feared the worst for me and for Becky. I envisioned the police coming to get me and carting me off to jail. Finally, I could hear footsteps coming up the stairs. The heaviness of each step told me it was my dad. I braced myself for another beating. Surely Dad would not flog me if I were asleep. I felt a playful twisting of my big toe. I acted groggy as I opened my eyes and looked at my dad. Dad bent over and sat on the bed and offered me a piece of cheese. That gesture signaled that peace might be possible.

Dad patted me on the back and said he was sorry he lost control in the yard. He told me that the BB had hit Becky just below the left nostril and traveled up her skin and lodged below her left eye. The doctor made a small incision and used tweezers to pull the BB out. Not even a stitch was needed to close the cut and no long-term damage was done. I was so relieved; my parents called her parents and they came to the hospital to get her. Dad said they were very upset but that they were handling it okay considering what might have happened. Dad agreed to pay all the medical bills.

The progression is obvious in this story. The tragedy to Becky could have been much worse. If this interceding incident had not occurred in my development, something much worse could have loomed on the horizon at the rate I was negatively progressing with my gun. I'm thankful it happened; it brought the metaphoric fence more tightly around me and I needed that to happen. Only God knows how my gun progression might have ended had the incident with Becky never happened.

Over our professional careers, we have witnessed thousands of times when so-called experts try to convince kids to behave properly or to make promises or threats about acting certain ways. Sometimes celebrities will be paraded forward to admonish kids to act morally, ethically, and legally. These methods sometimes work for short periods of time, but rarely work for long periods of time. One is left to ask what the solution is to getting kids to act in ways that are self-governing and self-regulating with regards to properly accepted behaviors. The answer is amazingly simple. The principle of Strategy 7 is the best way for kids to monitor their own behavior, and it does not require adult admonitions, nor does it advocate the use of threats or rewards.

The best way for kids to control negative behavior is for them to simply stop, reflect quickly about what they are about to do that is considered risky behavior, then to simply ask themselves the following question: *Am I willing to accept the consequences of what will happen to me if I am caught doing what I am about to do?* This question should be asked every time a person is tempted to smoke, chew, and dip tobacco; is about to use drugs; is about to hurt another person emotionally or physically; is about to perform an act of violence; is about to deface or destroy property; is about to engage in some elicit sexual activity; is about to perform a risky or dangerous behavior or activity; tempted to steal or be deceitful. Even seemingly harmless activities like speeding, gossiping, not wearing a helmet, not studying for exams, not doing homework, and undermining authority can also be corrected using this question.

Why do humans act in such silly, stupid, or destructive ways? The answer lies in understanding human nature. Humans are different from any other animal. We can think, we have emotions, we can reason, we can love, we can rationalize, and we can be tempted to act in ways that are both helpful and destructive to ourselves and others. All other animals, as far as we understand today, act on instinct only. What governs the behaviors of all animals except humans is reproduction and survival. Humans, on the other hand, have those survival needs but also have more profound emotional needs as well.

William Glasser (1990) lists the four basic emotional needs: to have fun, to have freedom, to be loved or to belong, and to have power. All of these needs can present huge problems for humans. The need itself is not deleterious, but the actions that lead to fulfilling these needs can be harmful or destructive. These emotional needs and the complex nature of the human brain create huge problems with human behavior. Every human being is capable of making serious mistakes. Religions all over the world are designed largely to worship but also to control the human "condition" of sinning as the Bible describes such behavior. It has been said that churches are not built for saints but rather for sinners.

One understands that humans digress from accepted norms and morals; one just has to hope these indiscretions are not so harmful or destructive that they end up destroying the person or his or her family. Obviously, there are degrees of harmful activities or behaviors on the part of humans, with some being more benign than destructive, but even these lesser negative actions can lead to more powerfully negative behaviors or actions later in life. Extrinsic factors can rarely affect how we act or behave—behavior control must come from within.

By considering whether you are willing to accept the consequences of what you are about to do you can very quickly reason through the latent scenario about being caught and the likely fallout. This is a huge deterrent to negative behaviors because it forces us to think before acting. This thinking process can interrupt stupid or destructive behaviors just enough to create doubt. Few people will want negative consequences doled out for improper behavior, so by thinking of negative consequences, one can actually control his or her own behavior. People have to understand that thoughts can usually control actions, actions control behaviors, and behaviors develop habits.

Bad habits can be destructive. By controlling our thoughts, we can control our actions and prevent behaviors that lead to unhealthy or unwise habits. This is where the critical question comes into play. Asking the question of Strategy 7 creates thinking that interrupts negative decision making. Kids and even adults can be very impetuous. They can act quickly with little thought about consequences. This lack of self-control of impulses many times separates those who are in jail from the rest of us. Nearly all humans think about behaviors or actions that can be harmful or destructive, but most of us can control these negative thoughts. By asking the question of Strategy 7 each time you are faced with doing something wrong, you can control yourself in positive ways.

We have found that thousands of students have benefited from this simple approach. It has been reported hundreds of times to us how students who have been educated to this simple thought process have used it to keep from getting into serious trouble. Even adults who have been educated to use the question of Strategy 7 report how it often keeps them from speeding or from doing some other minor indiscretion. The process of using Strategy 7 is a self-governing thought technique that not only keeps us from acting in extremely negative ways, but also monitors our actions.

We have numerous outstanding stories that illustrate how young people failed to control their impulses or behaviors and experienced tragedy or near tragedy. The stories below have been changed from original true stories to illustrate the point of Strategy 7. You should remember the message conveyed more than the story itself because the message emphasizes that we must all follow Strategy 7 to prevent destructive behaviors. Remembering only the stories without truly comprehending the message from the stories defeats the purpose of sharing these tragedies.

STORY I

On a warm drizzly fall Sunday evening, four high school students were riding in a car throwing eggs at houses. The two students in the back of the car were drinking and hanging out the windows, throwing beer over the top of the car onto each other. It was misting rain outside and the boys in the back seat were holding on to the clothes rack on the inside of the window so as to not lose their balance and fall out the window. Both boys in the back were drunk and having a great time. As the car pulled into a yard to heave eggs at the intended house, the driver, as a prank, quickly accelerated to spin the rear wheels to throw the boys off balance in the back. It was seemingly all in fun!

The car yanked violently sideways headed for the front shrubbery when the tires stopped the car as it hit the side of the cement leading to the house. The car stopped and the engine died briefly before the driver restarted the car and accelerated throwing dirt, sod, and water all over the front of the house. As the car bounced out of the yard over bushes and headed back to the street, all four boys were yelling in drunken delight. At just that moment, the boy on the right rear window had his extended arm torn off just above the elbow by a speed limit sign. The arm, with the beer bottle still securely fixed in the hand's grasp, fell to the gravel beside the road. The pole of the sign also knocked the boy unconscious. He then fell out of the car and banged violently to the ground, breaking his neck at the second vertebra. The back tires of the car also ran over one of his feet.

The car went on down the street for about a half block before the other boys realized the he had fallen out of the car. They pulled a U-turn and headed back still laughing until they saw his lifeless body crumpled alongside the road. At first they thought he was feigning being hurt until they saw his severed arm still clutching the beer bottle. As they jumped from the car, they all realized the grave nature of what had just happened. They checked the young man for a pulse, but none was found. One of the boys ran to the house whose yard had just been damaged to summon the police and ambulance personnel. Within 10 minutes the paramedics arrived. Although dead at the scene, the fatally injured young man was pronounced dead at the emergency room 15 minutes later. His blood alcohol content was 0.17.

The surviving boys eventually admitted to their destructive actions with the car and had to pay $3,000 each for the damage to lawns and property. Two of the boys were 18 and had to spend several nights in the county jail. The family of the boy that died sued the driver for $4 million. Thinking about the consequences of their actions could have prevented any of the tragedies that happened that night. The boys and their families all paid a dear price for their actions and their lives were changed forever. Every detail of what happened that night could easily have been prevented by a simple process of thinking through the consequences of their behavior before acting out their ill-fated behavior. Maybe then the boys would have chosen a more productive and superior path.

STORY 2

As a high school junior, Sean was a young man who sought out adventure in the wrong venues. For several weeks, he and his friend Mike had thrown eggs and tomatoes at cars and houses. Although they had come close to being caught on several occasions, the two delinquents were able to avoid detection. One evening in late September, as the tomatoes were overripened and rotting on the vine, both Sean and Mike decided to throw a few tomatoes at passing cars approaching the city on a two-lane state highway.

Both boys had taken turns and had thrown a half dozen with only two tomatoes hitting their marks. It was Sean's turn to throw the last tomato. He was standing between two large evergreen trees on the cement walkway leading to a small white house where two elderly people lived. The distance between where Sean was heaving the vegetables and the middle of the highway was only 30 feet. As the next car approached from the north, Mike yelled, "Here comes one, get ready." As the car approached, Sean stepped out far enough to clear the evergreen trees as he let go of the tomato. Out the corner of his right eye he noticed that Mike was running toward the alley that ran next to the house. Sean did a quick glance toward Mike and wondered why he was running. Just as Sean turned toward the car, the horror of his actions became totally apparent. The car was a state police vehicle and the tomato was headed toward the car at warp speed.

No sooner had Sean realized the gravity of the situation then the tomato struck its intended target beautifully. The red seeds and mush slammed into the post that held the windshield and the side window, painting the entire windshield and side area of the car completely a sloppy mess. No sooner had the tomato hit its mark than the sound of screeching tires and crunching gears could be heard. The officer had put the cruiser on its nose trying to stop immediately. Sean was terror stricken as his feet felt like they were buried in cement. He actually had to lift his right foot up to be able to move.

The patrolman had swung open the car door and had almost fallen out of the car trying to exit quickly. Sean finally was able to move in slow motion toward where Mike's shadow had blazed past him just a few seconds earlier. Now he knew why Mike had run. Sean was sprinting down the alley and couldn't even see Mike, who had doubled back toward his house where he would be safe. The patrolman was no more than 20 feet from Sean as they both bolted down the cinder alley. The officer continually yelled, "Stop, stop!"

Sean ignored the patrolman and continued for a block before he spotted a 3-foot chain-link fence framing a backyard. Sean thought he would leap the fence and head toward the Girl Scout woods in the distance. He figured the cop wouldn't be able to scale the fence and it would give him a safe distance to find a place to hide in the woods. Just as he scissored the fence and was about half way across the half-acre lot, Sean caught a glimpse of something leaping off the porch of the house that sat innocently inside the fence.

It was a huge male German shepherd that was sprinting toward Sean with teeth bared and positioned very low to the ground in a sprinter's form. The dog appeared ready to "eat" Sean just before he leaped head-first over the fence on the other side of the yard. Sean fell hands first onto the cinder alley, pounding his chin so hard it nearly blacked him out. His hands were full of the little black rocks and the stinging pain in his palms hit him immediately. He knew the cinders were lodged inside the skin of his hands, but there was no time to hurt.

A big one-acre lot stood between Sean and the safety of the woods and he was determined to make it there. Just as he traversed the lot and was headed around a house, he heard the officer scream, totally out of breath, "Halt or I will shoot!" Sean's life flashed before him as he slowed to a stop and saw the officer with his gun pointed in the air. Sean thought briefly about giving up. He imagined what it would feel like to be shot, how he would look in his casket, how his dad would react, what the papers would say, and if the football coach would be sad.

All of these thoughts, rushing at the speed of light, pounded his consciousness but vanished as quickly as they had appeared. Sean said to himself, "Keep running you fool!" He rounded a small house just feet from the woods and instinctively decided at the last moment to dive under a huge juniper bush in front of the house that faced the woods. The officer's view was momentarily blocked by the house, which gave Sean time to leap for cover. He scrambled up next to the base of the bush, and he wondered if any snakes were nearby. The maneuver worked or least it appeared to work! Sean lay shaking under the bush as he could see the patrolman move onto the hill at the base of the forest.

A street light illuminated the scene as the officer made his way into the brush and disappeared into the foliage of the woods. For a brief moment, Sean thought he would bolt and run back toward Mike's house, but thought it unwise to move from the seeming safety of the juniper. After a few moments, the officer made his way out of the woods just a few feet from where he had entered. He had his flashlight out and began looking in a car that was parked on the street. The officer then looked in trees and walked by the bush where Sean lay prostrate as he shined the light in toward Sean. The officer proceeded past the bush and Sean nearly fainted from fright. Briefly thinking he was "busted," Sean then gratefully witnessed the officer look in the basement window well of the house.

Sean could hear sirens in the distance and thought about the state patrol car still parked on the highway with the door open. What must people be thinking? Sean could no longer see the officer but was paralyzed with fear. For nearly 45 minutes Sean decided to lay still and not dare venture from under the bush. Finally, Sean eased out, vigilant to the potential danger. As he slipped to the corner of the house, he raised his head to see what lay ahead. He was relieved to see nothing but moonlit darkness. He could hear the dogs barking as he broke out in a dead sprint toward the mile distance to his home. He didn't stop running. His gait was like a crazed man running a military obstacle course. Sean avoided every headlight and obstacle as he made his way home.

Just as he arrived home, he slowed to catch his breath, as he felt covered with perspiration and fear still gripped his every bone. Sean gathered himself until he was composed enough to enter the garage door leading to the patio that adjoined his room. He quietly slipped into his bedroom and knew his parents were asleep because the house was dark and still. The only activity was his cat Cleo, who was purring and rubbing his leg as he readied for the safety of his bed. Sean slipped under the security of the covers, his heart still pounding.

The night was long and Sean did not sleep a wink because of the worry. What had happened to Mike? Did he give himself up? Did the police have forensic methods of finding the culprits? Sean began rehearsing lies that he could tell if someone confronted him in the middle of the night or at school the next morning.

The next day as Sean drove to school he could see a state police vehicle parked outside the school. Dread gripped him as he entered the school. Mike was waiting at Sean's locker with a huge smile on his face. Mike told Sean of the long commotion caused by the officer not returning his radio commands. It seemed the entire police force, ambulances, and fire trucks descended on the scene. Mike said officers were knocking on doors and asking neighbors questions.

Mike was lucky that his parents were in Las Vegas and so he didn't have to answer the knock on the door. He watched in awe as the carnival atmosphere continued for what seemed like an eternity. Sean said, "What about the state patrol car parked out front of the school?" Mike said, "What state patrol car?" Now both boys were scared and completely void of color as they scurried off to class. Both boys knew they were going to be called to the principal's office at any moment. At lunch, both boys noticed the state patrol car was gone and everything appeared safe.

No one ever discovered what happened that night and no real harm was done, but the fear and anguish caused by this incident taught Mike and Sean a valuable lesson about throwing tomatoes. Both found themselves wishing they could go back in time and prevent the potential debacle from ever happening. If only they had known about Strategy 7, they could have eliminated the angst and turmoil that haunted them for days.

This story points out the foolishness that permeates our society with young people trying to find fun and adventure in all the wrong ways and places. Our society is full of latent criminals—teens seeking to explore the limits and pushing the boundaries of acceptable behavior. These actions and behaviors usually are spontaneous or not well thought out with regard to consequences. Heeding the message of Strategy 7 can help everyone to avoid mistake-prone lives.

STORY 3

Millie, Darcy, Amy, and Alice were country joy-riding on a balmy summer evening after getting off work at a local restaurant. Millie was driving and the girls were trying to find the country home of a boy that Darcy had met at a dance a week earlier. The girls became hopelessly lost after taking several gravel roads trying in vain to find the residence. It was around 2:00 A.M. and Millie was worried that her parents would be upset that she wasn't home yet. This was before cell phones and pagers. Millie was driving over 60 miles per hour when she crested a hill on a gravel road.

As her car lights leveled out again, Millie realized she was at a T intersection with nowhere for the car to go but straight ahead, through a fence, and into a field of soybeans. She slammed her brakes as hard as she could and the rear of the Ford Fairlane began fish-tailing out of control. Suddenly the car leaped from the road, still traveling well over 40 miles per hour. The car became temporarily airborne when the automobile landed squarely on top of a cement mile marker that jutted out of the ground about 4 feet. The car stopped immediately and became impaled on the cement post. The sudden stop broke the steering wheel off and Millie's chest hit the center steering wheel column with a blunt force that took all of her breath away. The steering wheel broke off in a complete circle still gripped tightly in Millie's hands.

Amy was sitting on the front passenger side and was thrown up against the windshield, breaking it into thousands of tiny shards of glass. In the back seat, Darcy was behind the driver and was thrown over the top of Millie and onto the dashboard by the impact. The soft drink she had been drinking was now pouring out onto the front of Millie, who was trying frantically to breathe. Darcy was not hurt and she climbed awkwardly back onto the seat in the rear behind Amy. Alice was seated behind the front passenger and had braced herself with her feet on the front seat and was not hurt.

As Alice quickly exited the car to help the girls in the front seat, she glanced beside where she had been sitting and noticed the cement post was sticking up a foot through the back seat squarely in the middle of the seat. Darcy started crying and said, "Oh my God, if I had been just a few inches more toward the middle, I would have lost a leg or my life." Darcy then got out of the car and looked for a farmhouse to call for help. The nearest farmhouse was over a mile away. An ambulance came within 30 minutes.

Darcy couldn't call her parents or her friends because with the adrenaline rush, she couldn't remember any phone numbers. The police took her and Alice to the police station and called everyone's parents. Amy received 56 stitches to her forehead and arms but was released from the hospital early in the morning. Millie was taken by ambulance to the hospital. She broke her sternum and had punctured a lung. She remained in the hospital for 6 days. Her car was a total loss. Damage to the field and fence was $670.

This tragedy could have been prevented if these girls had simply thought about Strategy 7. These seemingly innocent scenarios are played out thousands of times daily all across the country. It is nothing short of a miracle that more tragedies do not occur. Young people as well as adults must learn to self-monitor themselves to avoid these types of accidents and tragedies. These girls were not thinking about what could happen to them if they continued to speed out of control in the country on gravel roads. They were fortunate not to have died, but the lessons learned have certainly stayed with them for a lifetime.

STORY 4

This story involves a young college couple on their way home from a football game. It was 10:30 P.M. and they were headed back to campus on a busy four-lane highway. A homeless hitchhiker was walking alongside the road as their car approached. The boy said to his girlfriend, "Watch this. I'm going to scare the hell out of this waste to humanity." With that, the boy tossed a half-empty beer can out of the car toward the man. The impact of the beer can traveling 60 miles per hour struck with full force on the homeless man's left eye and forehead.

Both saw the direct hit and laughed until they realized what had just happened and that there were cars on the road going the same direction behind them. As the two students raced onward, the girl turned to see the man slump to the ground. Their laughs quickly turned to dread as a car stopped to see what had happened to the homeless man. The stopped car was blinking its lights as if to tell the couple they saw what had happened. Fun turned to gloom as they both discussed what to do.

Finally, the girl pleaded with her boyfriend to go back to the scene. He refused to go back and continued on to his apartment saying that nobody would care about a homeless man and that no one had gotten his license number. However, within an hour, the state police arrived at his house. At first he denied even knowing anything about the incident, but his girlfriend began crying and told him to tell the truth. Incredulously, they quickly discovered that the homeless man had died from his injuries.

The girl was questioned numerous times but ultimately was not charged in the case. The young man who had thrown the beer can was arrested and eventually plea bargained for 4 years in jail with 4 years probation on a felony charge of involuntary manslaughter. He never graduated from college and now works as a roofer in his hometown. The girl married someone else and eventually graduated with a degree in elementary education. The attorney for the young college man in this story pleaded with the jury that the man did not understand the laws of physics and thought that the thrown beer can would simply scare the man walking along the highway and not hurt him in any meaningful way.

Physics dictated that the beer can tossed out the window hit the homeless man with a force equal to propelling the can at 60 miles per hour, making the can a lethal weapon. As is usually the case, ignorance is of little consequence when the law is the issue. This incident, which took less than a few seconds from the point of inception, completely ruined the promising future of an otherwise intelligent young man. If only the young man had just briefly thought of the potential consequences of his actions, he might not have committed this senseless act.

STORY 5: THE FINAL STORY

The final story in this sequence of stories involves two young eighth-grade boys riding their bikes home from a school dance on an October Friday evening. As the boys made their way over the interstate overpass, they stopped briefly to watch cars zooming by beneath them. Terrance said to Aaron, "Wouldn't it be funny if we dropped something off the overpass and it landed on the roof of a car?" Aaron replied, "Yeah, let's do it." Aaron then proceeded to the side of the overpass and saw a large section of a broken terra cotta drainage tile. The overpass was a seldom-used road, particularly late at night, so passing cars were a rarity at this time of night. Both boys parked their bikes beside the overpass near the cement bridge. They walked toward the middle of one side of the bridge overpass and were laughing with anticipation.

At no time did either boy even talk about a potential consequence that might occur as a result of their actions. Aaron handed the heavy cylinder to Terrance to heave over the edge. Both boys agreed it was too heavy to drop on a car. The intent was to simply create a hazard for cars to swerve to miss. Without looking to see what was coming, Terrance threw the block over the edge. Unfortunately, the block fell directly through the windshield of an oncoming mini-van. The van then careened out of control and slid off the road onto the grass median. As the van hit the side of a hill, it turned sharply back toward the road and began flipping sideways over and over. The van skidded into the oncoming traffic and was hit broadside by a semi loaded with steel wire. The impact slid the van over a hundred yards down the highway.

When the screeching sounds and dust finally cleared, the quiet was suddenly pierced with the agonizing screams of the van's occupants. Everyone in the van ended up dead—the father, mother, teenage daughter, and 6-year-old son. The large drainage tile had killed the father on impact and the subsequent crash killed the others. The young middle school students looked on in stunned disbelief. Fear gripped both boys as they jumped on their bikes and dashed for home. As the boys reached a departing place to their homes, they began rehearsing their alibi should anyone suspect it was them who had caused the tragedy. They hoped the occupants of the van would be okay.

Two days later as the news hit the newspapers and television, the police began putting together opportunity and motive, and started interviewing students at the middle school because it was learned that the middle school had had a dance and the route over the bridge and the timing seemed reason enough to investigate students. Aaron was brought down to the principal's office. He was so nervous during the police interview that he quickly confessed to what had happened. When the boys were asked why they did what they did, they both indicated they didn't want to hurt anyone, they just did it on the spur of the moment and didn't think about what might happen. Both boys were placed in a juvenile detention center until they turned 18. The carnage caused by their lack of thinking of consequences changed numerous people's lives forever.

Thousands if not millions of stories can be told to illustrate how certain behaviors can devastate people's lives in numerous ways. This book could not possibly even scratch the surface to illustrate how people rarely think of Strategy 7 in controlling behavior. The stories previously told are but a few examples of how people act impulsively without thinking through consequences and what will happen if they get caught or don't think before acting in certain harmful ways.

The following list of activities may tempt anyone at some point. These activities can be particularly troublesome and tempting to young people, but they are not limited to just students. The following behaviors and their potential consequences are offered as reminders of how young people should think about what can happen if they indulge or use any of these. The message for the person reading this book is to think rationally about the consequences offered and then to make the decision as to whether the consequences are worth the gamble of the action or behavior. If it is deemed worth the gamble, at least the person has thought through the consequences and chose to act rather than simply reacting to a situation or instance. Self-control is the only effective answer to these kinds of misdirected behaviors.

TOBACCO USE

Smoking, dipping, or chewing tobacco products can be negative in the following ways:

- The cost is totally prohibitive.
- The damage done to lungs, teeth, gums, and organs is tremendous.
- The narcotic effect of addiction to these products is well documented.
- Research confirms that these products shorten life spans.
- The social negative effects can be devastating to building relationships.
- These behaviors cause your breath, clothes, car, and home to stink.

Two demonstrations that are particularly effective in showing people the ill effects of tobacco use are:

1. Use a clean white handkerchief and blow a puff of cigarette smoke through the clean white cloth and note the yellow stain. The stain is nearly impossible to remove with normal washing.
2. This is nearly impossible to duplicate but a story to illustrate this experiment can be just as effective. Have members of the class pinch two separate lung specimens. Human lungs do not need to be used, but rather use large pieces of raw meat (which have

been placed in a location with continual exposure to smoke). Coal tar can be placed on one lung to represent the damaging effects of smoke on human lungs. Have the students pinch the tobacco lung specimen with their right fingers and the regular specimen with their left fingers. The right fingers will have a black tar film left from pinching the specimen that will not wash off with soap and water. It will require turpentine (or paint thinner) to remove the black tar substance from their fingers. The instructor should inform students that the regular lung specimen was a segment of lung taken from a 70-year-old male cadaver who had never smoked. This lung pinch will wash easily from their fingers. The first blackened looking piece of lung specimen (right fingers) will illustrate a 40-year-old woman who has died of throat cancer. She was a two-pack-a-day smoker and had been smoking since the age of 16. It is this right fingers lung pinch that will require turpentine to remove the stain.

We have also seen authority figures using disgusting pictures of mutilated people that had parts of their face, mouth, or throat removed from the effects of smoking or using smokeless tobacco products. We have found this method can also be effective in helping to control students' use of tobacco products. It is most effective if a living person can be used instead of pictures. This is usually next to impossible because people mutilated and scarred rarely make themselves available as freak shows.

UNDERAGE DRINKING

Underage drinking of alcohol can have the following negative effects:

- It is illegal.
- It can lead to drunk driving and the consequences of hurting yourself and others are obvious.
- Alcohol is expensive.
- Alcohol consumption can lead to addiction.
- Alcohol use can lead to alcoholism with medical, job-related, and family consequences.

- Alcohol use has been proven to age the body faster.
- Alcohol use can lead to liver damage.
- Alcohol use in excess can lead to birth defects.

The following tragic story is one of stupidity. Bradley was a 22-year-old recently married brick mason. On Labor Day, he and four other couples went to a state park reservoir in Illinois. The men drank all day long. At five in the afternoon, just prior to cooking hot dogs for dinner, Bradley's friend Rick announced he would challenge anyone to swim the 200 yards across the lake. If anyone made it, he would give him or her $20. Bradley didn't even respond verbally but quickly sprang to his feet and started sprinting to the edge of the water. Everyone just laughed and thought he was only joking around, but when he dove into the water, the laughs turned to nervous anticipation.

Off Bradley went, looking like Tarzan, with his near flawless form. Bradley swam methodically and seemingly effortlessly until about two thirds of the distance across, when he stopped to rest. Suddenly he turned and yelled that he was cramping and that he needed help. Every-one assumed he was feigning drowning as his wife walked toward him in the water as if she could jump stride the entire distance to rescue him; she knew he was in trouble, but she couldn't swim.

Suddenly Bradley slipped under the water and came up gasping for air. It still seemed like a joke to the rest when Barb, his wife, screamed to help him. The others looked for something to throw to him as Jim, his brother, dove in to try to rescue him. He didn't make it more than 30 feet before he realized he couldn't do anything to help. Bradley disap-peared beneath the water and the reality of the tragedy sunk in imme-diately. Everyone was running in different directions trying to get help. There were no lifeguards and no boats. Ellen, Jim's wife, ran to the guardhouse and summoned a ranger. He immediately called for help. The ambulance and fire trucks arrived within 20 minutes. Bradley's body was found within 30 minutes in 8 feet of water. The autopsy showed his blood alcohol level was .23 at the time of his drowning.

Another story involves a party of over 70 young adults. The party went well into the morning hours when several of the men decided to shoot at squirrels that were in the backyard. Paul, a 26-year-old recent father of a baby girl, owned a shotgun, but it was out in his car under the seat. He kept the sawed-off 12-gauge shotgun under his front seat of his

Honda Accord for protection. Paul carried large sums of money at times in his job as a closing clerk at a local supermarket. When Paul went to retrieve the gun, several people from the party followed him to see the hand-carved stock of the gun that Paul was bragging about. As he arrived at his car, he reached under the seat to pull the gun out; the gun was stuck.

Paul bent over to see what was creating the snag and pulled harder on the gun. The gun exploded in Paul's face as he was looking under the seat. The blast blew him back several feet. He was lying on the ground, face up, with his right eye and right cheek completely blown away. His hands came up to his face and just as suddenly they became limp and fell to his side. He was mortally wounded. The force of the blast blew buckshot and brain material into Paul's friend Sam's upper left leg. Sam fell to the ground screaming but sprang to his feet and ran to the house not knowing that his friend Paul lay dead.

Everyone in the house was only concerned about Sam until several others began screaming to call an ambulance, that Paul had been shot in the face. Paul's wife ran to his side and dropped to her knees. She was inconsolable. When the ambulances, fire trucks, and sheriff's officers arrived, Emily was treated for shock and a panic attack. Paul was beyond help. Sam was taken to Mercy Hospital and underwent several hours of surgery to remove the buckshot and to repair his badly damaged front thigh. This is yet another example of a tragedy that could have been avoided by simply thinking of Strategy 7.

Consider these headlines that could come from newspapers all across this country which have involved drinking alcohol:

- Two girls killed when car skids out of control on curve. The driver's blood alcohol content was 0.18.
- Four-time convicted drunk driver kills family of three in accident on highway.
- Man takes his wife's life after a night of binge drinking.
- Drunken woman runs over her husband after arguing outside an east side bar.
- Drinking teenager slips to his death from a cliff at the state park just north of the city.

ILLEGAL DRUG USE

The use of illegal drugs or the misuse of prescription drugs can lead to varying events, which might include addiction, jail time, family tragedy, a life time of disease or horrible symptoms, or even death. Drug abuse has been increasing in schools across the nation and has become commonplace in many high schools. It is critical that we, as educators, come to terms with this harrowing truth. The use of illegal drugs or misuse of prescription drugs involves the following negative connotations:

- Drugs are illegal and lead to felony convictions.
- Drugs can destroy the body.
- Drugs can destroy families and relationships.
- Drugs can devastate finances and lead to ruin.
- Using illegal substances can irreparably harm the brain.
- Reproduction difficulties and birth defects have been linked to the use of illegal drugs.

Many people think "recreational" drugs are harmless and should be legalized or the punishment should be reduced for those who are caught using such drugs. However, the evidence of harmful consequences beyond addiction, costs, family tragedy, and criminal penalties make using these drugs ill-advised.

One rarely explored convincing argument against drug abuse is for young girls to understand how getting high can damage their reproductive systems. Girls of all ages have inside their ovaries every egg that is capable of making a child. There are a finite number of eggs in each girl at birth.

When a girl gets high on drugs, uses alcohol, or smokes cigarettes, the effects are evident in every cell in the body, including these eggs the size of a small pin head. When a girl gets high or drunk, the eggs are high or drunk too. Irreparable damage can result to a single egg or all eggs by abusing drugs or alcohol. If this happens, the girl may conceive a deformed child later in life from a single earlier indiscretion. What a tragedy! We sincerely believe that if all girls were armed with this knowledge, most would make informed decisions in appropriate ways if they were educated to implement Strategy 7 in their daily thought processes.

VIOLENT BEHAVIOR

Violence can be detrimental in the following ways:

- Violence is against the law and can lead to prison terms.
- One never wins a fight.
- People hold grudges for a lifetime for some inflicted violence against them.
- Violence leads to more violence.
- Violence usually harms the body or property, and many times, irreparably.
- Violence can lead to injury or death.
- Violence can destroy relationships forever.

It seems as if violence is a part of our very existence today. One can read, watch television, play video games, go to movies, and witness firsthand acts of violence every day of our lives. These violent acts are an ingrained part of a democratic society. They surround us in ways that are nearly impossible to escape. These violent acts will eventually touch each of us to some degree in our lifetimes. The old cliche that those who live by the sword shall die by the sword is integral in understanding how destiny reflects reaping what one sows in terms of violent actions or behaviors. The following story illustrates this point.

Tony was a young man who had been a bully all 14 years of his life. His dad had constantly beaten him as a youngster for any little indiscretion. Tony grew up with a monumental chip on his shoulder and an attitude that could chill you on the warmest of days. Tony progressed through high school fighting anyone who got in his way or challenged his authority. It seemed everyone was afraid of Tony. During Tony's senior year, he hit a young man from a neighboring school in the eye with his fist. As a result, the boy lost his sight in that eye, and Tony spent 20 weekends in jail. The other boy had provoked the fight by throwing a foam cup full of a carbonated beverage over the hood of

Tony's car after Tony gave him the finger of disrespect. This incident was one of many that Tony encountered in his troubled youth. It seemed Tony was constantly the source of violent episodes.

Three years after Tony graduated from high school, he was driving down a hilly country road on his 750 Honda motorcycle. He was not wearing a helmet and was traveling in excess of 80 miles per hour. Tony believed he was invincible. He had yet to be in any sort of automobile or motorcycle accident and had oftentimes been the reason behind other people's unfortunate events. After increasing his speed to nearly 95 miles per hour, a car nearly sideswiped him as he crested a hill. Tony was so angry at what had just happened that he lifted his fist in the air and turned to make an obscene gesture at the driver. As he turned back, his bike left the side of the road and hit a telephone pole head on. The bike's front tire missed the pole but the rest of the bike hit full force.

Tony was thrown into the wooden pole. The force of the impact flipped Tony around the pole and back onto the road. He was killed instantly. He was so badly mutilated that his body could not be shown at the mortuary. Tony died as he had lived—violently. It is an unfortunate, but rather enlightening story. Tony was a violent individual who had been inflicted with emotional and physical abuse since his days as a young child. As a result, Tony knew nothing but violence and sadness.

ADDICTIONS AND ADDICTIVE BEHAVIORS

Addictions that are or that have the potential to be damaging are:

- Alcohol
- Drugs
- Prescriptions
- Sex
- Shopping
- Lying
- Cheating
- Stealing
- Obsessive/compulsive behaviors
- Love

The best way to avoid addictions is to control one's thought processes that lead to actions and behaviors that result in the development of negative habits and addictions. Controlling our thoughts can prevent most addictions. It is as simple as that! A conscious thought process is also the reason why Strategy 7 works so well in controlling negative behaviors and actions.

In summary, this chapter outlines the difference in tragedies—those that we can prevent and those that may lie beyond our individual control. Understanding what leads to tragedies is essential to understanding how to control our actions and behaviors for a better life free of misery and torment. By understanding and thinking about consequences before we act we can create success in our lives. This conscious thought process is what controls our behavior and actions. Understanding this simple concept can move or prevent mountains of obstacles to success in life.

9

DISCIPLINE IN SCHOOLS AS THE FOUNDATION FOR ALL LEARNING

There is no discipline in the world so severe as the discipline of experience subjected to the tests of intelligent development and direction.

—John Dewey

Chapters 2 through 8 outline the seven strategies for success and how teachers and administrators can use these strategies to develop their own personal strategies in an effort to motivate their students to be successful. We have added this chapter as a sourced reference for teachers and administrators to look at the "big picture" of school discipline. The readers of this book can then begin to formulate their own personal, philosophical framework as they develop strategies to promote success in students from the unique perspective that all educators bring to the profession.

Some of what is included in this chapter will appear redundant and repetitious. The reason for this repetition of ideas and philosophies is that the strategies we espouse in this book are all research-based in principle and proven through years of practical experience. When we look at discipline in schools, we must understand that without a research-based approach, the entire system of educating our youth will ultimately fail. An effective disciplinary approach is not just a required ingredient, it is the foundation for building a great educational system in which to teach students to be great students and productive adults.

> I've come to the frightening conclusion that I am the decisive element in the classroom. It is my personal approach that creates the climate. It is my daily mood that creates the weather. As a teacher, I possess a tremendous power to make a child's life miserable or joyous. I can be a tool of torture or an instrument of inspiration.
>
> —Haim Ginott

This quote can be interpreted both positively and negatively depending on perspective. We believe this quote beautifully illustrates why it is imperative that schools initiate a positive system of discipline.

Discipline differs markedly from punishment and threats in several noteworthy ways. Discipline is not punishment nor does it ever involve threats. Punishment and threats have no place in schools either in words or deeds. These two words conjure up thoughts and perceptions of a lack of control over consequences, negative connotations to reactions, perceptions of injury to the body and soul, and a perception of a power struggle between the weak and powerless versus the strong and omnipotent. Punishment and threats are almost always negative and rarely are effective over the long term. School personnel are no different from parents in the need to use discipline to manage behavior and attitudes. However, the use of punishments and threats must be avoided at all times. Discipline is highly positive; punishments and threats are usually not constructive.

The following passage from an article that appeared in the March 2004 issue of *Phi Delta Kappan* magazine puts punishment in perspective.

> Punishment, another coercive approach (to discipline), is based on the idea that a student has to be harmed to learn or be hurt in order to be instructed. The truth is that people do best when they feel good about themselves, not when they feel bad. Punishment is counterproductive to a teacher/student relationship because imposed punishment (whether called natural or logical) immediately prompts negative feelings against the person meting out the punishment. Punishment satisfies the punisher more than it influences the punished. (Marshall & Weisner, 2004, p. 501)

In many ways, the breakdown in discipline in the home, community, and schools is partially to blame for a decline in our social structures, which directly affect how well public schools operate. It is not uncommon to see cameras, surveillance equipment, padlocks, fencing, and other intrusive structures in place to protect our students in public schools.

Bobby Knight, the former basketball coach at Indiana University and now coach at Texas Tech, makes the comment routinely in his speaking engagements that kids have not changed over the past decades, but rather "we" have changed. Meaning, kids just reflect what their caretakers allow them to do. Knight also routinely states in his philosophy that sports are, in some ways, the last vestige of discipline in our society, outside of the military. Whether one agrees with Knight's assessment, the fact remains that kids are growing up faster, are exposed to many more outside influences, are exposed to violence and sex at a much earlier age, and routinely commit heinous acts against property and other human beings.

An excellent book titled *Rampage: The Social Roots of School Shootings*, by Katherine Newman (2004), does a wonderful job of exposing the nuances behind the troubled youth that commit heinous acts of violence in our nation's schools. Newman and her Harvard graduate student coauthors cite several factors that contribute to this malady of destruction: (1) The students live on the margin of acceptable behavior in school through their extracurricular activities and peer groups; (2) over half the students had been bullied or been called names prior to the shootings; (3) these students are often plagued by individual problems such as family dysfunctions, or they suffered from some form of mild to severe mental illness; (4) reasons given by these students for their heinous actions include being mistreated by their peers, doing something considered "manly," trying to send a message to those left behind, creating a warped sense of fame, attempting to advertise their actions prior to the actual event, and planning an elaborate rampage; (5) about two thirds of these troubled students routinely flew under the radar of school discipline. There is usually evidence of a downward spiral, of violent writings, of giving either subtle or outward threats as to their actions, yet not necessarily giving any outward indication to their parents that they planned such actions; and (6) these students had access to guns either through home or some other source.

So although not all troubled students fit into some neatly packaged predictor of future action, several common ingredients do surface in most instances. By understanding these commonly shared traits or tendencies, school personnel can begin to intercede early enough to make positive changes. Clearly, the problem with troubled kids is complex and deeply rooted in our society. The problems go far beyond the school setting. The adults in schools can, however, have a powerful impact on how students view themselves and others. This chapter will delve into the solutions behind these efforts.

Presently, schools are being forced to use instructional practices that encourage discipline problems by doing more busy work in the classroom, exposing students to more rote methods of learning, placing students into competitive learning environments, and teaching students passively, rather than actively. The material presented is often not relevant to students, boring in nature, and has little meaning in a student's life. Long gone are the days when kids came to school eager and willing to learn, regardless of instructional strategies.

Nowadays, kids expect to be entertained and wowed in the classroom, instead of longing for knowledge. Teachers find themselves needing to be performers and givers of instruction versus facilitators of instruction. Discipline in schools is interwoven with instruction practices that are based on sound, research pedagogy. Doing things the effective and precise way in the classroom will go a long way to running an efficient and disciplined school environment. We are doing it all wrong and we will give suggestions on how to do it right in this chapter.

William Glasser (2000) and Phillip Schlechty (1997) both have written about how schools must produce quality "work" in order for all students to achieve and grow. They both indicate in their writings that the biggest problem with discipline in schools is the level of work that students undertake. Both say that rote learning, worksheets, memorization exercises, endless answering of end-of-chapter questions, Socratic questioning, passive learning activities, and other mundane learning tasks actually contribute to discipline problems.

Students get bored with their "work" and do not persist in completing the work or immerse themselves deeply enough to get any meaningful growth from the activity. We agree that this problem can contribute greatly to discipline problems in school, which can also lead to a decline in quality learning opportunities for students. However, there is much more to this complex problem than just merely improving the quality of "work" those students undertake.

In Rachel Kessler's (2000) book titled *The Soul of Education*, she laments the fact that we are not nurturing in children very important affective domain dispositions. Unless properly fed, the body of a child will not grow. Similarly, the mind will not develop unless it is inspired. And the spirit will not endure if it is not nurtured (Kessler, 2000). This is not about a religious soul but rather a moral soul that lives within all of us that yearns to be nurtured so that we can be better people, better citizens to our brethren, and better human beings. When schools nurture the spirit and soul of students in highly positive ways, the vale of discipline begins to evaporate and what schools are left with is a climate of love and caring. This enlightened thought is one of the most basic foundation blocks in building a great school.

We have over 40 years combined experience working in public schools as teachers, assistant principals, principals, superintendents, university teachers, and authors. Through this vast framework of experience and buoyed by a solid research foundation, we give insights in this chapter into what has not worked and what will work in creating disciplined school climates that are conducive to learning and improvement.

Negative behaviors or actions tend to beget more negative behavior if left unchecked. This often leads to more serious problems as the child continues to push the envelope further until stopped by someone or some event. Positive behaviors and actions will also grow students in profoundly positive ways. As educators it is imperative to keep negative behaviors and actions to a minimum by instituting effective disciplinary systems. Conversely, it is also imperative that schools nurture and encourage students to grow cognitively and affectively so that the exponential features of learning can "kick-in."

One can examine nearly any heinous crime and see the behavior that could have been avoided. Therefore, by avoiding this behavior, the crime could have been prevented. For example, a young child may start by stealing from his parents or siblings; soon the stealing moves to friends or neighbors, who may not "prosecute" the child in any serious way. If left unchecked, this behavior could then proceed to breaking into houses, then easy target businesses, and then possibly escalating into armed robbery. The robbery can then turn violent when the person encounters someone who challenges them. If the child were remediated in this behavior when it first appeared, positive growth would have resulted. Left unchecked, it grew into a monster that threatens the very fabric of our civility.

A specific example might be a child who experiments by smoking a cigarette in middle school. This child may progress to smoking nearly every day if his or her behavior is not checked. Left undiscovered, the child may soon be smoking 10 or more cigarettes a day and may well develop a bad health habit that can be extremely addictive. Massive amounts of research have linked teenage smoking, early marijuana use, and later use of harder drugs. That same body of research says that students who routinely use marijuana at an early age will often experiment with more dangerous drugs later in their lives, oftentimes leading to a life of despair.

Harold Schoenberg once said, "Anybody who gets away with something negative will come back to get away with a little bit more the next time" (Thinkexist.com, 2006). John Wooden once said, "He who lives without discipline dies without honor" (Thinkexist.com, 2006). Without a doubt, discipline, when implemented properly, is an essential part in developing limitations and boundaries in a person's life. Discipline is positive because discipline is the key to stopping and escalating negative behaviors and actions.

Therefore, it is crucial that one keeps the metaphoric fence locked tightly around oneself (in terms of negative growth through the use of proper disciplinary systems both in schools and in the homes). The consequences meted out through discipline stops bad behavior before it escalates into something that creates a scar on the person or society. Discipline sets boundaries of acceptable behavior by implementing procedures of consequences that are steeped in progressive increments of seriousness.

As important as discouraging negative behaviors is in developing young people, encouraging positive growth allows students to grow in profoundly positive ways. Teachers and administrators must allow and encourage the widening growth of this positive metaphoric fence that surrounds a person by using discipline to teach students proper behavior, attitudes, and habits, so that the child will search out and grow in new avenues. For example, by encouraging and rewarding positive behaviors in students, they learn that positive dispositions can enrich their lives. Discipline plays a huge part in both scenarios. The absence of discipline can corrupt any individual, and the presence of discipline can help one to grow positively. In either case, discipline is a highly positive term that indicates nothing but positive growth in students.

Discipline is one of the most misunderstood words in our society, but particularly in schools. Discipline comes from the word "disciple," which means "to teach or teacher." When one disciplines, one simultaneously teaches; when one teaches, one can grow in overwhelmingly encouraging ways. Therefore, one "disciplines" to facilitate growth in positive ways and to inhibit one's growth in negative ways. Legally and morally, schools have more than a right to discipline students and children; they have an *obligation* to discipline. By ignoring bad behavior or turning one's head when something negative happens, one actually can hinder the holistic growth of a child. When one ignores, one condones; and, when one condones certain acts or behaviors, one is left to live with the negative behavior or attitude.

Discipline is a highly positive word, one that everyone should embrace and not reject. Society should welcome discipline because it teaches us boundaries of proper and accepted social behavior. Without discipline, the world would be chaotic, unorganized, and a criminalistic place to live. Civilized people must have accepted disciplinary strategies and procedures so that all people can live freely, safely, and in an environment conducive to positive growth.

As we view discipline from a traditional, legal standpoint, a legal phrase has routinely framed how schools administer discipline. Schools differ markedly from the real world of legalese. There is a Latin phrase that defines the role school personnel play with regard to disciplining students—*in loco parentis*. Translated, the phrase means literally "in place of the parent." In other words, once parents agree to send their children to public schools, they give near equal legal rights to the teachers, administrators, and school staff as if they were the parents of the students. The courts through laws and court precedents have routinely given this right to all school personnel for over a century.

Many parents have a difficult time understanding what this means both practically, theoretically, or legally; but this legalese Latin phrase is a fact of life in administering schools. Judges, courts, and school personnel recognize that it would be nearly impossible to run schools without this fundamental legal tenet. Additionally, this fundamental right of schools to discipline students cannot be usurped or given away.

Just like in the home, teachers, administrators, and school personnel (including bus drivers, custodians, aides, and cafeteria workers) have an *obligation* to discipline students to create and to maintain a safe and productive school environment. Parents exercise the same duty with their children in order to run a functional household. Employers should exercise the same duty with their employees in order to ensure a safe and productive working environment. Simply put, school personnel have pretty much the same legal rights toward students that parents exercise with their own children. As long as the discipline relating to a student is considered reasonable to an objective person, then there is a legal obligation on the part of school personnel to act accordingly to keep the school running smoothly, efficiently, safely, and effectively.

But more importantly, students benefit from a positive disciplinary system in schools. Students grow in profoundly positive ways when discipline is used properly. Parents that "fight" with school personnel because they believe their child's rights have been violated risk the danger of alienating the very people who want to help their child grow in positive ways, to stop the potential proliferation of a negative behavior, and to teach students proper behavior in a civilized world.

It is always better to make a mistake in disciplining a student who is innocent as opposed to not "catching" a student when they do something wrong. With proper counseling, the first case can be a positive learning experience; in the second case, the student runs the risk of escalating the negative behavior. Reasonableness replaces probable cause in schools, as does guilty until proven innocent on infractions (when reasonable safeguards were followed) versus innocent until proven guilty in the real world.

With reasonable suspicion, teachers or administrators can act decisively. They do not need permission from parents to search, investigate, or interrogate a child who is reasonably suspected of doing something that breaks a strategy or law. This is discipline and it should be viewed in a highly positive light.

Without question, schools must have discipline to teach students correct behavior and to ensure their success in life. There is more to discipline in school than merely meting out a certain consequence for a certain act; it involves an entire climate that encompasses an environment that is welcoming and nurturing to every child. Once the teacher/administrator understands this basic premise of understanding how to nurture students to be successful in school/life using an effective disciplinary program, then these same teachers/administrators will begin to understand the next phase of building the foundation necessary to build a beautiful and long-lasting structure for learning.

RESPECT AND RAPPORT

Two incredibly important words must be developed and then nurtured in our schools for the necessary climate to be present to facilitate authentic learning: respect and rapport. Building a climate of mutually satisfying respect on the part of the student and the adults in the school is a basic foundational concept. The other basic foundational concept is building rapport among students and the adults in the school. Both respect and rapport are essential to the success of educating students. If either is missing, learning will be jeopardized.

One builds respect by never singling a student or adult out for negative criticism. This should always be done in private even when the temptation may be to take immediate corrective action. Another concept that is often overlooked and vastly misunderstood is that you should rarely, if ever, single another person out in front of his or her peers for positive recognition. This has the potential to ruin the "chemistry" in the classroom/school. People simply want to belong and to be accepted (Glasser, 1998). By singling people out with negative or positive comments, you are attempting to remove these students from their peer group. When you do this with negative comments, the student will often elicit subtle support from others in the room.

Other students will often identify with the student being singled out and surreptitiously strike back at the teacher thinking this could happen to them as well—a "circling of the wagons" mentality. The student being negatively singled out will many times defy the teacher and refuse to learn after such incidents. This becomes an aberration to the teacher. Teachers and administrators abhor this behavior in students. By criticizing in private, peers are not involved and the ego can be preserved. Teachable moments happen when disciplining privately.

The same is somewhat true in praising positively in front of peers. The praised student will often subconsciously try to regain the group's acceptance by not performing to the praised level or may simply not perform to the praised level for fear of being abandoned by his or her peers. The peers of the praised students often feel neglected and as if they have simply been overlooked. They may begrudge the praise heaped on another student.

The same human personality traits apply to teachers and other adults. We recommend limiting *all* criticizing and praising to private venues. If no peers are present, then public praise can be extremely helpful, but neither should be done in front of peers. Even one violation of this premise can irreparably harm the respect one earns with students, teachers, and other adults in the school setting.

Rapport is nothing more than relationship building. In schools, rapport is simply making a concerted effort to get to know students and adults personally, without getting personal. Assuaging a particularly tough situation using the correct measures breeds rapport with students. By asking nonpersonal questions of students and adults, one can ascertain many positive facts about the person, which can lead to profoundly positive relationships. For example, a teacher can ask students about extracurricular activities, parents, siblings, and so forth. By questioning without being invasive, a teacher can build strong bonds.

Various items that teachers and administrators should learn about students are their names, their parents names, their brothers and sisters names, what part of town they live in, grades in various subjects, likes, dislikes, hobbies, pets, goals, future plans, and similar noninvasive questions that help you understand that person better. These questions and similar ones can be asked at opportune times and not all at once, which has the potential to scare or confuse students. Using common sense is critical here. Always remember that it takes valuable time to build rapport or demonstrate mutual respect—no professional should operate under the assumption that two incredibly important concepts can be achieved overnight.

Another way to build respect and rapport is saying hi in some way every single day every single time you see a student you know. Then say goodbye in some way every time a student leaves your area. Smiling is another way to make students feel welcome. A handshake, high five, low five, or other similar harmless ways to reach out can be effective as well. Although hugs and touches can be highly motivational, professionals must be very careful and discreet as to how and what is acceptable. This can vary greatly with different students and adults. Saying thank you, you're welcome, pardon me, I'm sorry, have a nice day, goodbye, how can I help you, and other similar niceties go a long way to build rapport and support respect in and around the classroom.

Demonstrating sincere empathy is another way to build rapport and respect. Putting "emotional deposits" into people's emotional bank accounts (Covey, 1990) is another excellent way to build respect and rapport with students and adults. Giving positive, nonpersonal messages to students and other adults also works well in building rapport. Developing personality traits that are positive, caring, and encouraging work well in developing strong interpersonal relationships. These comments create a climate of trust and trustworthiness.

Following these simple suggestions works not only for teachers and student relationships, but also for administrator and teacher relationships. In fact, these suggestions will work well in any interpersonal relationship as long as there is no overt or underlying temptation to want something sinister from a relationship. The rest of this chapter will illustrate these suggestions in a sourced format.

> Young people need good models not critics. No written word nor spoken plea can teach our youth what they should be; nor all the books on the shelves. It is what the teachers are themselves.
>
> —John Wooden

Lorraine Monroe (2003) is the author of several books and articles on the subject of building a positive school climate from a "bosses" perspective and also from a leadership perspective. Lorraine was a school administrator in the Bronx, New York. Her "Monroe Doctrine" is emphatic about how all children respond to people who care about them. She talks about schools being a safe haven for children, where they know that there is an adult waiting for them to help them succeed in school and life. In other words, Monroe talks about how the affective domain of human relationships is the foundation of all learning. Without this foundation of mutual respect and rapport building, little else matters until these ingredients are evident throughout the fabric of the school environment.

James Comer (2004) writes about the three critical ingredients that are necessary to develop students in a holistic approach to learning: relationships, relationships, and relationships. In other words, the answer in helping students to grow in behavior and cognitive terms is for them to build strong relationships with the myriad people who surround them on a daily basis. When relationships flourish, learning naturally follows. Building strong interpersonal relationships is synonymous with building rapport.

In Comer's article for the *American School Board Journal* in April 2002, he writes:

> Understanding how kids develop and respond to challenges is the first step in understanding their behavior. . . . The "no-look, no-smile" child had had bad experiences with adults at home—many in and out of her life, some abusive. She didn't trust adults. But with a caring, positive, responsible teacher, she finally smiled. (Comer, 2002, p. 31)

In this same article, Comer points out that continuity, trust, and support all were critical ingredients in helping students' behaviors. With improved behaviors comes academic growth as well.

In Harry Wong's (1991) book *The First Days of School*, he expounds at length in several chapters on the need for positive discipline in the classroom, the need for positive dispositions of the teacher, the need to use research-based techniques, and the need to follow procedures when students break the strategies.

Wong advocates: having a school-wide discipline plan that minimizes disturbances and maximizes learning; a well-ordered environment and high academic expectations; using both general and specific strategies with clear-cut rewards and consequences for following or not following the established strategies; treating students with dignity and respect; good discipline by treating people the right way and teaching the right way; making people feel good about themselves; allowing students to act responsibly; teachers and students acting courteously in all interpersonal relationships; dressing professionally; greeting students daily with positive expectations and a smile; great communication among students and their parents; learning students' names as fast as humanly possible, and then greeting the students daily using their first names; a well-managed, well-structured classroom where preparation makes for a well-run classroom; having a work-oriented climate with no confusion, no wasted time, and no disruptions; showing a genuine love of each child; creating an inviting atmosphere for students; and a mentally and physically safe environment in which students can feel free to learn unabated.

Jim Fay and David Funk's (1995) book, *Teaching with Love and Logic*, goes right to the heart of how we must understand children if we are to be effective in managing how they act, behave, and learn. Once we understand children's needs and what motivates them, the result is a collective good for the entire school environment. Both the individual student's feelings about how he or she is being treated and disciplined as well as the attitude of the adults in the building are important. Fay advocates: giving students input into the strategies; allowing students to help construct consequences of breaking strategies; and giving students choices in consequences. But at all times, Fay advocates we must first love kids unconditionally and then use logic in managing their behavior in highly positive ways.

In our nation's public schools, it is not unusual for schools to label students with a disability if they do not perform or behave to the expectations. According to the 1998 U.S. Bureau of Census, 25.5% of African Americans and 27.1% of Hispanics live in poverty. That same year, only 8.6% of white children lived in poverty.

Since the research stated in early chapters suggests that achievement is closely tied to the income level of the parents, then much of the criticism leveled at our public schools should be directed at society problems and not so much at problems within public schools (Rothstein, 2004). Presently, there is a disproportionate percentage of students from African American and Latino heritages that are labeled as mildly mentally handicapped (Brandt, 2000). The evidence appears to suggest that if these two groups do not learn at the same rate and cannot perform to a subjective level on standardized tests, then they must have some mental disability that explains the discrepancy from one group to another.

Sean Covey took his father's book titled 7 *Habits of Highly Effective People* and applied the same principles to teens. Sean Covey's (1998) book is titled 7 *Habits of Highly Effective Teens.* Teachers should learn the habits listed in his book so that these success traits can be taught to students. These habits form a backdrop for effective schools as well. Covey says that teens (schools) must be proactive, have an end in mind, prioritize what is important, create win/win situations in interpersonal relationships, do a better job of listening with their hearts, cooperate, and work smart by continually improving. If students and schools can develop these important traits, discipline in schools will improve, and the climate of the school will improve in the same measure.

Clearly, the foundation of all great classrooms and schools is the ability to get students in a mental frame of mind that is conducive to learning. Intrinsic motivation is the key to attaining this frame of mind. That motivation is only possible if the students respect the teacher, want to learn from the teacher, and allow the teacher to enter into what Glasser (1990) calls their quality world. When students enjoy good rapport with their teachers it fosters an attitude where the student cares about the teacher, and the setting is then created for an effective learning environment. If any of these factors are missing, students may actually defy the teacher to teach them anything.

To achieve this necessary environment, we suggest that schools develop meaningful and productive disciplinary procedures that promote the growth and well-being of all the individuals in a school environment. When students and teachers are treated the right way and for the right reasons, meaningful school reform will follow. We suggest building strong interpersonal relationships among all members of the school family. When schools reflect these dispositions, the foundation of effective achievement will surely follow.

As we close this chapter, we encourage you to develop your own personal teaching format to teach the seven strategies for success based on the knowledge and insights gained in this book. That process will then become part of a strong foundation of understanding when coupled with a comprehensive mindset of how to treat students to create an environment and climate of optimal learning. Once the foundation is properly set in place, then what will follow is a profoundly positive setting where students can reach their individual potential and lead highly successful lives.

CHARACTER AND SUCCESS

Character building begins in our infancy and continues until death.

—Eleanor Roosevelt

Success is a journey, not a destination.

—Ben Sweetland

Many authors have tried to define character and its effect on human success in life. If you were to examine the literature on the subject you would find numerous character words that are universally accepted as positive character traits. Since no one author has a market on the subject of character traits or development, we will take a few of the universally accepted common positive character traits and discuss how this book builds on these traits. Although some experts may agree or disagree as to what constitutes positive character, the fact remains that there are universally accepted traits that nearly any reasonable person would consider as worthy of inclusion in any discussion on positive character.

As the title of this book suggests, the seven powerful strategies, when properly presented by teachers/administrators and learned by students, can have a significant impact on positive character development. When one examines the strategies individually, one might ask how these strategies alone can promote character building in students. We believe that character development is not nearly as complex as some experts would have us believe.

Through our extensive educational experience working with literally thousands of school-aged students, it has become apparent that once students begin changing their behaviors and attitudes in positive ways, the results are exponential in nature. The success a student experiences as he or she begins practicing the seven strategies leads to even greater positive results. We have often witnessed an awakening of sorts on the part of students. Some would like to see a resource proving that these strategies work when taught properly and with love and caring.

As with many new ideas and concepts, the solution can be extremely simple. Once one sees the solution to any seemingly complex problem, many times, one is shocked by the simplicity of the answer. So although no proof exists beyond anecdotal experience that the seven powerful strategies work to help students to succeed and to build character, the proof of over 10,000 successful students is reason enough to trust that this approach really works.

Although not a true random sample in a scientific sense, when you start to experience the effects of this approach on the lives of a true cross section of all conceivable student types—from special education students to juvenile delinquents, to gang members, to ordinary students, and to gifted students—the results will nearly always be the same. Students, once a metaphoric mirror is placed in front of their faces for them to see the truth revealed, will begin to change.

We sincerely believe that *every* student wants to succeed in school and become successful in life. No one wants to be miserable and unsuccessful! Unfortunately, many students and adults lead lives that make them miserable, and these same people often appear helpless to change the direction their lives are taking. We have seen firsthand the transformation these seven strategies have had on students. Positive character development is simply a byproduct of changing behaviors, attitudes, and actions that lead to success in school and in life.

The national Character Counts! movement in this country lists "Six Pillars of Character" (Josephson, 2000): trustworthiness, respect, responsibility, fairness, caring, and citizenship. Although other authors on the subject of character education may list more character traits, these six concepts reflect the heart of changing a student's character.

Trustworthiness simply means that others can trust that one will make good decisions, be honest in correspondence with others, tell the truth whenever appropriate; in short it means a person can be depended upon to do things in the right way and for the right reasons. Every strategy listed in this book has a direct or indirect link to this concept. Therefore, when one practices the seven strategies outlined in this book, one is developing this positive character trait simultaneously.

Responsibility is critical to building independent students who can function in the real world long after their formal education has ended. Without responsibility, a student often flounders in life with no clear purpose or motive. When a teacher/administrator instructs students how to demonstrate responsibility in highly responsible ways, success inevitably follows. When success follows, this character trait is reinforced to an even higher level. Being responsible simply means understanding consequences of actions, understanding discipline and its role in personal development, and understanding that whatever you sow you reap. Therefore, when one practices the seven powerful strategies, one is developing this positive character trait simultaneously.

Respect is given much narrative space in this book. The mutual nature of respect among students and adults is paramount to building strong, positive relationships. When one respects oneself and others, positive character is developed and revealed in those demonstrating this concept. Many educators and parents often try to teach this concept using various methods and lessons, but we have found the best way to teach this concept is to use stories and examples so a student can reflect on past actions to construct new behaviors that reflect proper treatment of others.

Fairness can appear subjective at times, depending on perspective. However, when examining this concept more closely, one can determine a rubric of objectiveness in defining this seemingly difficult to define term. Fairness means that one acts in objective ways in all situations. It does not mean that flexibility is not allowed, but rather there is consistency within a fact-driven framework of observation.

Students will often see teachers treating some students differently in class or singling out certain students for attention (either positive or negative), and this can lead to a perception of unfair treatment, particularly with students who routinely demonstrate negative behavior. Because some students by their very nature take more of a teacher's time in the classroom, when these same students appear to get worse treatment or better treatment, depending on the perspective of the person looking at the scenario, the appearance of unfairness comes into play.

In this book, we have pointed out that when one discusses with a student the various reasons why teachers might view other teachers differently, the concept of fairness comes into focus, and students begin to see that not everyone is the same, and differences in how teachers interact with students is expected and necessary. Students who are taught these lessons begin to accept that much of what is happening to them is under their control. Once students feel empowered to change for their own benefit, positive character begins to manifest itself in all their attitudes and behaviors.

Once again, the concept of caring appears in nearly every book on effective teaching, learning, or climate building. It is a foundational concept that must be present in all classrooms and schools for students to develop and become successful, responsible adults. Teachers/administrators must reflect caring in all they do; they must project this to all who enter their doors; they must teach to students this critically important concept; and they must teach their students with an air of understanding and rapport building in mind. All coercion, sarcasm, threats, punishment, mean-spirited, and negative actions must be eliminated in schools for students to see the proper modeling of caring and its profound effect on people.

Citizenship is covered extensively in this book in several of the espoused strategies. Students must learn the difference between being a good citizen and pleasing their peer group or "friends" who do not understand the power of good citizenship and the effects this concept has on everyone's lives. Good citizenship and democracy go hand in hand. For democracies to work effectively, they are dependent on a citizenry that promotes everyone's common good. Schools must promote common ground and common good principles in everything they undertake (DuFour & Eaker, 2005).

Although this list may not be exhaustive, most lists that one encounters on character education will have obvious overlaps and synonymous traits. Many states have adopted character education codes or laws. To use one as an example, Indiana has legislation passed in 1937, 1975, and 1995 that dictates what schools must teach to students. Here is a list of what Indiana mandates as good citizenship instruction (Indiana Code 20-10.11-4-4.5):

1. Being honest and truthful.
2. Respecting authority.
3. Respecting the property of others.
4. Always doing one's personal best.
5. Not stealing.
6. Possessing the skills necessary to live peaceably in society and not resorting to violence to settle disputes.
7. Taking personal responsibility for obligations to family and community.
8. Taking personal responsibility for earning a livelihood.
9. Treating others the way one would want to be treated.
10. Respecting the national flag, the Constitution of the United States, and the Constitution of the state of Indiana.
11. Respecting one's parents and home.
12. Respecting oneself.
13. Respecting the rights of others to have their own view and religious beliefs.

You can see from this example the expectation for the public schools to teach character education. This list demonstrates that citizens are concerned about character education and its effect on the future of this country.

Many students are not *taught* character education, even though many states mandate it be done. Why? There is no policing on this mandate, and with the growing reform movement on standardized testing and standards' instruction, little time is left to include these teaching traits as separate curriculum items. Even when these character traits are taught in school as an integrated curriculum, the concepts often elude even the most gifted and astute students. Therefore, when a teacher practices the seven strategies of this book, he or she is developing this positive character trait simultaneously in students.

Teachers and administrators have a moral and sometimes legal obligation to teach character to students. If one neglects this vital foundation of teaching students how to be successful in school and in life, then some students will never *know* what it takes to be successful because no one truly taught them how to do it.

Ed DeRoche and Mary Williams published a book in 2000 titled *Educating Hearts and Minds: A Comprehensive Character Education Framework*. They give tips for teachers and leaders, offer up standards for curriculum, show how to build consensus, how to create a nurturing climate in the classroom/school, delineate steps to develop a values driven curriculum, list ways to integrate character teaching into extracurricular activities, give advice on staff development, and also demonstrate how to assess the character education program. As one reads their book, you see how the seven strategies outlined in this book complement the message these authors promote. We believe that the teaching of the seven strategies should come first before any academic program is implemented. When we taught the seven strategies, the success students had, academically, seemed to follow hand in hand. Students want to succeed for a teacher or administrator who has taken the time to teach students these seven strategies. Students foresee the positive outcomes and can foreshadow the infinite possibilities they present.

Ann Lockwood's (1997) book on character education remains a good source for teachers and administrators in their pursuit of teaching character education. With a team of experts assembled who give meaningful input into the dilemmas facing character education in public schools, Lockwood is successful in demonstrating how schools can teach character education without infringing on religions and the diverse aspects of ethics and values that may not be universally shared and know if a character program is working or even exists in reality.

Although this book is timeless, the strategies outlined in here are not controversial and work without any broad implementation program. Every teacher and administrator can teach the seven strategies easily and without sacrificing the critical time required to teach the hundreds of standards each grade requires. The strategies listed in this book can be easily taught in as little as 2 hours total classroom time. Of course if a lengthier time frame is committed, there is a better chance of success with all students. Our approach is less than 4 total hours of instruction. This is well worth the time and the results will be evident almost immediately.

Tim Rusnak (1997) has also written on character education. His contributions have been largely on promoting leadership support through policy and practice of these programs, empowering teachers, demonstrating empathy with students, teaching self-control and self-discipline, and defining values and traits needed in each school. Rusnak's book also does a great job of demonstrating the comprehensive nature of character education and melds well with the message in this book. Many overarching ideas are evident in Rusnak's book and this book. Rusnak's book takes a more school-wide approach, whereas this book attempts to focus on one-on-one relationships, individual behavior, and so forth.

Sandra Davis-Johnson (2000) also wrote at the height of the current character education movement that has contributed greatly to the field of character education. Her book focuses on the imperative to give positive feedback to students to reinforce certain behaviors and to modify negative behaviors with consequences (a behavioralist approach). She also gives insights on how to handle students with emotional issues. Her systematic approach for younger students has shown great promise largely due to the success of behavioral modification. There is also a chapter on the rights of students, families, and teachers.

Davis-Johnson's approach to character education can work and remains the most widely accepted approach to behavioral modification to breed good character development. We believe our approach in this book to be much more effective with students. Students seem to have (and want) more control over their behavior and consequent actions. The choice to behave appropriately and to use the seven strategies espoused in this book are usually used more effectively by students because students are more likely to cognitively make the choice to behave a certain way.

Character education in schools involves everyone from the parents, to administrators, to teachers, to coaches, and to the community at large. When one starts with students and the seven strategies, in time all the other groups fall in line because eventually everyone will serve in those roles at later dates. The key to changing people is to start with children because all children eventually become adults. When one learns proper behaviors, actions, and attitudes at an early age, these tend to stay with children throughout their school careers and into their adult lives.

In 2001 the Josephson Institute of Ethics revealed some alarming statistics concerning the need for character education. These are some of the findings.

- Over 90% of parents and teachers believe students will benefit from teaching character education.
- Of 15,000 surveyed 13- to 17-year-olds, 40% of the males and 30% of the females admitted stealing from a store in the past year.
- In this same survey of the same students, 71% admitted to cheating in school.
- In this same survey of the same students, 16% said they had been drunk at least once in the past year.
- This same study revealed that 68% had struck someone in anger.
- The same study surprisingly showed little remorse for their actions with a whopping 91% satisfied with their own character and ethics.

Although this survey is not indicative of all students across a wide spectrum of locales and socioeconomic conditions, it does speak volumes about how students are behaving and that their views of themselves do not reflect reality. That is the reason this book is so important in reaching students. All students must be taught how to behave and act as the citizens in this country expect all people to conduct themselves. We have the experience and past practice to definitely say that what is offered in this book will work in changing how students behave, act, and think.

BRINGING IT ALL TOGETHER

The difference between a successful person and others is not a lack of strength, not a lack of knowledge, but rather a lack of will.

—Vince Lombardi

This book is dedicated to helping all students achieve success and promote positive character during their educational careers and posteducational opportunities. The seven strategies espoused in this book are unique in that they are not the same old enervating methodologies offered in other books. The approach is a novel approach to motivate students to succeed by empowering them with knowledge, successful strategies, and relationship-building techniques.

This book differs from most because it approaches changing behaviors, actions, and thoughts from a student perspective and not from a teacher behavior point of view. We are instructing teachers/administrators not only the "what" that must be taught, but also the "how" to teach the strategies in highly effective ways using the best research (see Appendix C).

We do not give advice on methods to correct behavior but rather give enlightened insights into how to empower students to act differently to avoid misbehavior. That concept is much more effective because it puts the responsibility back on the student in a powerfully seductive way.

These strategies empower the student with knowledge by giving them the necessary guidelines to become successful in school and in life. Success with some students is often no more than an evanescent thought that seems to elude them. Because *every* child wants and craves to be successful, nearly all students will take the information offered in this book and use it to transform their lives.

In Appendix A we provide wallet/business-sized cards for the students to use as a quick reference guide to the strategies. This card can be copied and laminated by the reader and given to students after the teaching is complete; this way the students will always have the strategies close at hand until they have mastered them as habits.

Also included in Appendix B is a quick reference guide for teachers and administrators to use until the strategies are mastered. Lastly, Appendix C was added to the book so that teachers/administrators can see how we have chosen to teach the seven strategies over the years. This implementation guide has proven successful for us time and again.

The strategies advocated in this book not only work, they can make profound differences in students' lives. Even teachers and administrators can improve their own character traits and everyday behaviors once they begin to see how students benefit from their teaching. Simply put, *everyone* benefits.

Getting on the road to success and staying on this path is incredibly simple. Of course it takes hard work and effort, but the formula is not difficult to grasp or to implement. All one has to do is religiously follow the strategies outlined in this book. Some changed dispositions may be witnessed immediately and others will take weeks to manifest themselves in students' behaviors and attitudes. The educator must be patient and dedicated to the principles outlined in this book so that students are given time to adapt to their awakening knowledge. Within a relatively short period of time, educators will begin to see students experiencing success and happiness.

Teachers/administrators must believe in the power of these strategies so they can teach them with confidence; teachers/administrators must be vigilant to their continued use in their class or school; teachers/administrators must be assiduous to model what hard work can accomplish; and teachers/administrators must stay on course, be patient in their implementation, and in about 2 months miracles can happen (Braden, 1993). Let us review the seven strategies:

- *Strategy 1*: Make critical distinctions in success terminology.
- *Strategy 2*: Build strong interpersonal relationships.
- *Strategy 3*: Avoid bringing negative attention to oneself.
- *Strategy 4*: Use positive body language to promote success.
- *Strategy 5*: Practice small, positive behaviors and actions.
- *Strategy 6*: Practice "mirror relationship building."
- *Strategy 7*: Learn to understand and accept consequences for one's actions and behaviors.

There they are! Simple! Direct! Easy to understand! Effective! Proven! Now the educator must figure out his or her own unique methodologies to convey these strategies to students. The teacher/administrator can use the seven strategies for success talk/discussion format or use another method to teach these strategies. The trick is to get this information to the student in a format that students will accept and persist in implementing.

The nice thing about following these strategies is that it only takes about 6 to 8 weeks for the new practices to develop into positive lifelong habits (Braden, 1993). Once new habits are entrenched in our daily lives, success will predictably and inevitably follow.

To help educators anticipate questions the students will invariably ask, we list here a few questions students may ask once the teacher or administrator has successfully conveyed the strategies to promote success and build character. These are commonly asked questions from our own students that are probably similar to those you will encounter. The answers shown below represent the common responses that we have given to the students.

What if I continue to practice these strategies and nothing seems to be happening? Keep following the strategies. They are working. You just may not be seeing outward results. Give them time. Nothing of any significance can be easily changed in just a few days. Most importantly, don't give up. One more pump when the arm is exhausted and the water may start to flow. Patience is the operative word.

Eventually, you will be visited by students who are greatly appreciative of the time and effort it took for you to teach them these strategies. The students, oftentimes, do not see the full working potential of these strategies until they have been given time to fully implement the strategies into all facets of their lives. This is when the changes truly take place.

Students will often ask questions about the implementation of the strategies. The following is a short list of questions one might be asked, as well as a few helpful hints on how to properly address their concerns.

After practicing the strategies, I can see teachers looking at me differently—is this normal? Absolutely! Depending on the depth of your unmotivated behavior, the more surprised the teachers or administrators will be in the turnaround. This is a sign that the strategies are working. Should the teacher be skeptical of your newfound motivation, use it to your advantage by doing subtle deeds to reinforce your new behaviors.

You might even suggest that the student speak individually with the teacher in question. Communication could be the key to opening doors in their professional relationship.

I have never been successful (motivated). Will I be able to handle what lies ahead on this uncharted path of success? Of course! Success is the American dream. Every American has the right and skills to become and do whatever they want. Rarely is talent the prohibitive factor in any success story. Attitude, hard work, and resolve will win out in nearly all success stories.

How will my friends treat me if I appear to be a Johnny-be-good, a brown noser, or a goody-two-shoes? Do not worry about this problem. If these strategies are followed correctly, your friends will not be able to discern any real differences in you with the interpersonal relationship you develop. The nice words you say to your teachers can be done in private venues. The affirmative nodding of the head and other positive body language messages will most likely not be noticeable to your friends. By modeling how to treat others, you will influence the behavior of your friends without being pushy or condescending. By understanding and accepting consequences, you will keep yourself and your friends from serious trouble, and that is good for you and your friends.

Will I see a difference in my relationship with my parents? Absolutely, no question about this! Your success is their success. When they see you happy, they should be happy, too. Following these seven strategies will develop strong relationships with your parents as well as all adults you encounter interpersonally. In short order, you will begin to see a profound difference in the relationship you have with your parents and extended family. Even your relationships with your siblings will dramatically improve.

How long will it take to change my habits? This is an excellent question that many people wonder about when it comes to changing behaviors, addictions, and habits. Some students give up way too soon. From years of practical experience, we have noted that it generally takes 6 to 8 weeks of concerted effort to change an old or form a new habit (Braden, 1993). The best advice is to mark on a calendar the date you begin your venture of practicing the seven strategies. Then mark 8 weeks out on the calendar to check your progress. If at any time you see that you are not following the strategies, refocus and add the days at the end to keep the focus at 8 weeks.

If you are serious about wanting to change, 8 weeks should create significant character and personality changes. Setting measurable goals that can be met daily will help you to stay focused on your changes. Every 2 weeks, these goals should be adjusted to reflect growth and fine-tuning. Try it—you will see positive, distinctive changes in your personality and character.

HOW TO IMPLEMENT THE SEVEN STRATEGIES IN YOUR SCHOOL OR CLASSROOM

Please see Appendix C for more implementation details.

1. Become totally familiar with all seven strategies and how they work to empower students to be successful.
2. Determine the best way to convey the teaching of the strategies. Make sure the students understand the "why" and the "big picture" reasons and be clear about articulating your motive—to help students succeed in school and in life.

3. Teach the strategies to endure learning using proven authentic methods of instruction. Check for understanding through authentic assessments.
4. Practice the strategies yourself so that you become totally immersed in the power of the strategies.
5. Continually revisit the strategies with students every time a situation comes up when particular students may slip back into bad habits. These become teaching moments.
6. Perfect the imparting of this knowledge each year.
7. Enjoy the fruits of your labor.

THE BEGINNING

The purpose of this book is to spread the knowledge of how students can easily change their daily habits in profoundly effective ways to ensure success in school and life. Although the strategies shared in this writing work well with difficult students, these same strategies have been demonstrated to be just as effective with all students. We have offered advice and wisdom to young people that require little effort and a short implementation time.

We are truly confident that the effectiveness of these simple strategies will affect young people for generations. Why? Because the message is historical, universal, and timeless. This means the strategies have worked in the past; they will work in the future; they are effective around the world; they will never cease to be effective in helping students to become better students and contributing citizens.

A final note: Teachers and administrators must understand how to and the importance of remaining pliant to the needs of individual students. This adaptable response to myriad behaviors on the part of supervisory adults is critical to understanding that people are complex creatures, yet nearly all will respond very predictably to positive feedback and the actions outlined in this book.

We wish the best of luck to you as you pursue the dream of motivating all students to become successful in school and in life. We also wish you all the tremendous joy of watching students build positive character traits in their daily lives.

Appendix A

STUDENT WALLET CARDS
WITH STRATEGIES SUMMARIZED

Here are examples of what we give to students as wallet cards after hearing the success strategies talk.

DR. BROWER'S SUCCESS TALK

The Power of . . .

1. Making Critical Distinctions
2. Building Strong Relationships
3. Avoiding Negative Attention Toward Oneself
4. Using Positive Body Language
5. Giving Positive Tokens of Appreciation to Others
6. Practicing "Mirror Relationship Building"
7. Understanding and Accepting Consequences for Actions

IST DAY TALK WALLET CARD

7 Powerful Success Strategies

The Power of . . .

1. Making Critical Distinctions
2. Building Strong Relationships
3. Avoiding Negative Attention Toward Oneself
4. Using Positive Body Language
5. Giving Positive Tokens of Appreciation to Others
6. Practicing "Mirror Relationship Building"
7. Understanding and Accepting Consequences for Actions

MRS. KELLER'S STRATEGY TALK

7 Powerful Strategies to Remember

1. Make Critical Distinctions
2. Build Strong Relationships
3. Avoid Negative Attention Toward Oneself
4. Use Positive Body Language
5. Give Positive Tokens of Appreciation to Others
6. Practice "Mirror Relationship Building"
7. Understand and Accept Consequences for Actions

Appendix B

TEACHER REFERENCE NOTE PAGE

IMPLEMENTING THE SEVEN POWERFUL STRATEGIES: A QUICK REFERENCE GUIDE

Strategy 1: Make Critical Distinctions

- Maturity Versus Immaturity
  Example story:

- Ignorance Versus Stupidity
  Example story:

- Listening Versus Hearing
  Example story:

- Threats and Punishment Versus Discipline
  Example story:

- Tattling Versus Being a Good Citizen
  Example story:

- Definition of a Friend
  Example story:

Strategy 2: Build Strong Interpersonal Relationships

Example story:

Strategy 3: Avoid Bringing Negative Attention to Oneself

Example story:

Strategy 4: Use Positive Body Language

Example story:

Strategy 5: Practice Small, Positive Behaviors and Actions in Interpersonal Relationships

- Always say hi, goodbye, and give a friendly smile to all adults one encounters on a daily basis
  Example story:

- Always limit comments to positive ones
  Example story:

- Leave some token of appreciation for the teacher
  Example story:

- Random acts of kindness
  Example story:

Strategy 6: Practice "Mirror Relationship Building"

Example story:

Strategy 7: Understand and Accept Consequences of Actions and Behaviors

Example story:

Appendix C

IMPLEMENTATION GUIDE AND STRATEGIES

These talks with students have been given titles to hype the expectations of what is coming. Building the suspense to a crescendo can be very beneficial to the talk's impact on students. We have spent several minutes before beginning the talks to share with the students how the talks have helped transform kids over the years; we may even share the story of Joe or other similar success stories to set the stage for what is to follow.

You are encouraged to develop your own style, presentation format, time constraints, stories, vignettes, examples, and teaching methods to suit your own personal needs.

TIME

We teach the seven powerful strategies to build character and promote success by breaking the teaching of these strategies into four 50-minute classroom periods. We sometimes will take less time than this or may require more time. It seems the more often we give the talks, no two ever turn out exactly the same. You will find the same to be true as you develop your own techniques in conveying the strategies to your students.

Early in our careers, when the strategies were being taught and the stories were fewer in number, all seven strategies could be taught in as little as 1 hour, but over the years, the stories have grown and the time allotted has reflected the new material. Even though the message behind the seven strategies is critically important, transmission of these strategies is not time dependent and should never exceed a total of 5 hours.

During the third and fourth days at the beginning of a given term, we will deliver our first two, 50-minute talks. This combined 2-day talk is titled "My Famous First Day Talk," even though the talk does not start until the second or third day of class. This is done to ensure that any class schedule changes will have most likely been completed and most class rosters set. This is very important since even one student missing the "talk" can have negative consequences as the term progresses.

During the last week of a given term, or thereabout, we give the second segment (talk). It involves two, 50-minute classroom periods. This two–classroom period segment (talk) is titled "My Famous Last Day Talk."

It is not essential that teachers wait until the end of the term to give the last segment, but we have discovered that there is too much material to cover in a short period of time. Also, giving reflection time on the first segment allows for the concepts to "soak in." By waiting until the end of the term, the students have something in which to look forward.

PARTS OF THE TALK

Here is how we break the entire talk into four parts covering all seven strategies.

- Strategies 1–3: Day 1 for approximately 30 minutes to 1 hour.
- Strategies 4–6: Day 2 for approximately 30 minutes to 1 hour.
- Strategy 7: Days 3 and 4 or approximately 50 minutes to 2 hours.

The reason the last strategy takes much longer to present is because this strategy is basically a new subject from the previous six. It also deals with behaviors that can get students into serious trouble in school, with their parents, or with the law enforcement agencies. Many more stories are told and the stakes are much higher with the last strategy. As you begin to use your own teaching strategies to present these concepts, you, too, will discover that the last strategy is the one that students can more easily identify with and consequently puts them in a wonderful frame of mind to pay close attention.

FORMAT

The format for each session is a mixture of: talk, discuss, tell stories, use vignettes, use analogies, lecture, tap emotions, summarize, notation type of teaching strategy. At some points, students enter into a discussion format. Sometimes the teacher/administrator will have the student think of his or her own stories and even write down those experiences that reflect the strategies being presented. Students are encouraged at times to summarize what they have just learned by putting their reflections into their own words. Stories and vignettes are powerful aids in teaching concepts as well. As Robert Marzano (2003) points out in his book for the Association for Supervision and Curriculum Development, two of the top-10 most effective strategies for enduring learning are the story and the analogy. Summarizing is also one of the top-10 most effective ways for students to learn new material.

If the reader hypes the subject matter and builds the talk up before it actually happens, the students will look forward to the talk and be in a better frame of mind to listen closely. Nearly all teachers and administrators practice theatrics in front of their classes—these topics are critically important to a student's success, so special attention to the presentation is paramount.

What the teacher/administrator will discover after their first talk is that all students will respond if the teacher/administrator follows up the talks with occasional reminders of what was discussed as certain pertinent items pop up during the course of a given term. When Dr. Brower was a high school principal, and now as a superintendent, he gave the talks to entire classes at one time in an auditorium setting. He has given this talk to as many as 1,200 students at one time with similar results.

In contrast to the large group setting, when classrooms with smaller numbers are available, teachers can implement small group instruction, cooperative grouping, writing personal vignettes to share with classmates, acting out potential scenes that illustrate strategies, and many other proven ways to instruct so that learning takes place with enduring quality. As Sergiovanni (1992, 1994) states in his writings, helping students to learn using proven methods coupled with a caring atmosphere will do wonders for changing students in positive ways.

Not only will the climate of a teacher's classroom be transformed in profoundly positive ways, but an entire school or school district can be transformed in similar ways. The quality of the presentation is critical to the message's success, but any teacher with the benefit of proven teaching strategies and with adequate preparation can make tremendous strides with students and how they succeed in school and in life.

REFERENCES

Braden, V. (1993). *Mental tennis: How to psych yourself to a winning game.* Toronto, Canada: Little, Brown.

Brandt, R. S. (2000). *Education in a new era.* Alexandria, VA: Association for Supervision and Curriculum Development.

Breaux, A. L. (2005). *The poetry of Annette Breaux.* Larchmont, NY: Eye on Education.

Comer, J. P. (2002, April). Why children do what they do. *American School Board Journal, 189*(4), 30–33.

Comer, J. P. (2004). *Leave no child behind.* New Haven, CT/London: Yale University Press.

Covey, S. (1990). *Principle-centered leadership.* New York: Simon and Schuster.

Covey, S. (1998). *7 habits of highly effective teens.* New York: Simon and Schuster.

Danforth, S., & Smith, T. J. (2004). *Engaging troubling students.* Thousand Oaks, CA: Corwin.

Davidson, J., & Davidson, B. (2004). *Genius denied.* New York: Simon and Schuster.

Davis-Johnson, S. (2000). *Seven essentials for character discipline.* Thousand Oaks, CA: Corwin.

DeBruyn, R. (2005). *The most powerful statement you can make to students.* Manhattan, KS: Master Teacher.

Deiro, J. (2004). *Teachers do make a difference.* Thousand Oaks, CA: Corwin.

DeRoche, E., & Williams, M. (2000). *Educating hearts and minds: A comprehensive character education framework.* Thousand Oaks, CA: Corwin Press.

DuFour, R., & Eaker, R. (1998). *Professional learning communities at work: Best practices for enhancing student achievement.* Bloomington, IN: National Education Service.

DuFour, R., & Eaker, R. (2005). *On common ground.* Bloomington, IN: National Education Service.

Fay, J., & Funk, D. (1995). *Teaching with love and logic.* Golden, CO: Love and Logic Press.

Gholar, C., & Riggs, E. (2004). *Connecting with students' will to succeed: the power of conation.* Thousand Oaks, CA: Corwin.

Glasser, W. (1990). *The quality school.* New York: Harper Perennial.

Glasser, W. (1998). *Choice theory.* New York: HarperCollins.

Glasser, W. (2000). *Counseling with choice theory: the new reality therapy.* New York: HarperCollins.

Harris, S. (2005). *Changing mindsets of educational leaders to improve schools: Voices of doctoral students.* Lanham, MD: Rowman & Littlefield Education.

Josephson, M. (2000). *Character counts!* Los Angeles: Josephson Institute of Ethics.

Josephson, M. (2001). *Survey.* Los Angeles: Josephson Institute of Ethics.

Kaplan, H. R. (2004). *Failing grades: How schools breed frustration, anger, violence, and how to prevent it.* Lanham, MD: Rowman & Littlefield Education.

Kessler, R. (2000) *The soul of education.* Alexandria, VA: Association for Supervision and Curriculum Development.

Lockwood, A. (1997). *Character education: Controversy and consensus.* Thousand Oaks, CA: Corwin.

Marshall, M., & Weisner, K. (2004, March). Using a discipline system to promote learning. *Phi Delta Kappan,* 85(7), 498–507.

Marzano, R. (2003). *What works in schools: Translating research into action.* Alexandria, VA: Association for Supervision and Curriculum Development.

McEwan, E. (2003). *10 traits of highly effective principals: From good to great performance.* Thousand Oaks, CA: Corwin.

Monroe, L. (2003). *Monroe doctrine: An ABC guide to what great bosses do.* New York: Public Affairs.

Nelson, G., ed. (2005). *Breaking the learning barrier for at-risk students: Practical strategies for dramatic results.* Thousand Oaks, CA: Sage.

Newman, K. (2004). *Rampage: The social roots of school shootings.* New York: Basic Books.

Northey, S. (2005). *Handbook on differentiating instruction for middle and high schools.* Larchmont, NY: Eye on Education.

Orange, C. (2004). *44 smart strategies for avoiding classroom mistakes*. Thousand Oaks, CA: Corwin.

Purkey, W., & Novak, J. (1996). *Inviting school success: A self-concept approach to teaching, learning and democratic practice*. Belmont, CA: Wadsworth.

Reider, B. (2004). *Teach more and discipline less*. Thousand Oaks, CA: Corwin.

Rice, Y. (2004, August). Seeking true definition of success [Electronic version]. *Decatur Daily*. Retrieved December 13, 2005, from http:www.decaturdaily .com/decaturdaily/religion/columns/.

Roffey, S. (2004). *The new teacher's survival guide to behavior*. Thousand Oaks, CA: Corwin.

Rogers, B. (2004). *How to manage children's challenging behavior*. Thousand Oaks, CA: Corwin.

Rosen, L. (2005a). *College is not for everyone*. Lanham, MD: Rowman & Littlefield Education.

Rothstein, R. (2004). *Class and schools*. Washington, DC: Economic Policy Institute.

Rusnak, T. (1997). *An integrated approach to character education*. Thousand Oaks, CA: Corwin.

Schlechty, P. C. (1997). *Inventing better schools*. San Francisco: Jossey-Bass.

Sergiovanni, T. J. (1992). *Moral leadership: Getting to the heart of school improvement*. San Francisco: Jossey-Bass.

Sergiovanni, T. J. (1994). *Building community in schools*. San Francisco: Jossey-Bass.

Sergiovanni, T. J. (2000). *The life world of leadership: Creating culture, community, and personal meaning in our schools*. San Francisco: Jossey-Bass.

Smink, J., & Schargel, F. (2004). *Helping students graduate: A strategic approach to dropout prevention*. Larchmont, NY: Eye on Education.

Stone, R. (2005). *Best classroom management practices for reaching all learners*. Thousand Oaks, CA: Corwin.

Theobald, M. (2005). *Increasing student motivation*. Thousand Oaks, CA: Corwin.

Thinkexist.com. (2006). Quote by Harold Schoenberg. Accessed February 16, 2006, from http://en.thinkexist.com/quotes/harold_schoenberg/.

Thinkexist.com. (2006). Quote by John Wooden. Accessed February 16, 2006, from http://en.thinkexist.com/quotes/john_wooden/.

Tileston, D. W. (2005). *Ten best teaching practices*. Thousand Oaks, CA: Corwin.

Whitaker, T. (2003). *What great principals do differently*. Larchmont, NY: Eye on Education.

Winograd, K. (2005). *Good day, bad day: Teaching as a high-wire act*. Lanham, MD: Rowman & Littlefield Education.

Wong, H. (1991). *The first days of school*. Sunnyvale, CA: Harry Wong Publications.

Yecke, C. P. (2005). *The war against excellence: The rising tide of mediocrity in America's middle schools*. Lanham, MD: Rowman & Littlefield Education.

ABOUT THE AUTHORS

Robert Brower is superintendent for the North Montgomery Community School Corporation in Crawfordsville, Indiana. Hs is also a consultant and presenter for many educational issues, including discipline in schools, teaching on the extended period, leadership topics, decision-making philosophy, building professional staff capacity, and teaching for learning. He has also published articles in numerous professional journals on these topics and is recognized nationally as an expert on trimester scheduling for both middle schools and high schools. His educational career has included teaching and coaching for 22 years, 6 years as a high school principal, and 4 years as a public school superintendent. He is coauthor of *Transformational Leadership and Decision Making in Schools* (2005).

Amy Keller works at Avon High School in Avon, Indiana. She is a freshman biology and zoology teacher and department chairperson. She also serves as the school's improvement cochair working with school committees to improve upon achievement at every level. She graduated from Indiana State University in Terre Haute, Indiana. After spending 2 years at Indiana University Law School, she decided to pursue a master's degree in school administration. Since then, she has completed her K–12 administrative certification from Ball State University.